STAR

Leadership Behaviours
for Stellar SME Growth

WILL MCKEE
JOHN MCKEE

Published by
OAK TREE PRESS
19 Rutland Street, Cork, Ireland
www.oaktreepress.com

A catalogue record of this book is
available from the British Library.

ISBN 978 1 904887 23 2

Printed in Ireland by ColourBooks.

CONTENTS

An SME is a small or medium size enterprise employing up to 250 people.
EU definition

It ain't what you do, it's the way that you do it,
It ain't what you know, it's the way that you use it,
That's what gets results.
From Bananarama lyrics, MCA Music, 1989

Leadership is the art of accomplishing more than the science of management says is possible.
General Colin Powell

AUTHORS

One of Ireland's most experienced board directors, Will McKee (www.willmckee.ie) is chairman of Linkubator and works with a broad range of corporations. From small start-up businesses to large established multi-nationals, and across an extensive range of manufacturing and service sectors, he trains and coaches chief executives and top teams. His competence comes from a rigorous business education and over 30 years of hands-on entrepreneurial experience of enterprise growth and early-stage business support in Ireland, Britain and North America in the roles of CEO, director, or chairman of significant companies in a wide variety of sectors.

John McKee is chief executive of Linkubator (www.linkubator.com) and CEO of Amtec Medical. John holds a BSc in Business Administration and Computer Science and an Executive MBA, both from Queens University, Belfast. He has been directly involved in three innovative start-ups and has extensive direct experience of assisting local NI aspiring entrepreneurs in international selling skills.

Will and John are father and son, business partners, colleagues and best friends, and have the privilege of working together to help owners, boards, CEOs and top teams to grow their companies.

Will's business career spans 40 years, and his extensive general expertise is enhanced by John's technical knowledge and ambitious energy.

Linkubator (www.linkubator.com) is a consulting company focussed on 'helping business leaders' in both the private and the public sector. Its specialist areas of expertise are:

- Strategy.
- Leadership.
- Selling.
- Entrepreneurship.

ACKNOWLEDGEMENTS

The germ of the idea for this book came from overhearing a remark on the lack of business literature directed at SMEs. The comment was made to Chris Howell, Chairman of City & Guilds, by Tracy Meharg of Invest Northern Ireland. Thanks, Tracy.

John and I are involved directly in a number of businesses in addition to our consulting activities, so to say that our days are full is an understatement. But we thoroughly enjoy the work and the opportunity to meet with many interesting entrepreneurial people.

But that doesn't leave a lot of free time for writing books while giving adequate attention to our families, so our main thanks, entirely from the heart, go to Mary and Jane, whose long-suffering patience allowed us to get on with the project.

Speaking of long-suffering patience, we cannot forget our publisher, editor and friend, Brian O'Kane, who endured five years of trouble and tribulation to get us to this point. His guidance, while firm and direct, invariably was right and delivered with a graciousness for which we are grateful.

Moving on from long-suffering patience to stoic endurance, we want to thank our close business colleagues and friends, Andrea Hay and Ian Cargill, without whose support we certainly would have been unable to keep all these spinning plates in the air.

Many other people helped us, too numerous to name individually but not too numerous for us to remember with gratitude. Our warmest thanks to all of you.

The most rewarding aspect of working on this book was in seeing positive leadership behaviours from the perspective of reality, using real stories of real people facing everyday challenges.

We had the privilege of sharing directly in many of these experiences, and observing the authentic behaviours, of courageous risk-taking entrepreneurs. The wealth-creating leaders we name in this book, together with many others from whom we have learned over the years, deserve the thanks of all for their vital contribution to society.

We salute you. We thank you.

Will McKee
John McKee

INTRODUCTION

This book is written to help executives in small and medium-sized enterprises to understand the STAR leadership behaviours that distinguish STAR leaders from average performers.

Will and John McKee, father and son, business partners, colleagues and best friends, have the privilege of working together to help owners, boards, CEOs and top teams to grow their companies. Will's business career spans 40 years, and his extensive general expertise is enhanced by John's technical knowledge and ambitious energy.

We have started, managed, grown, bought and sold many businesses of our own; often with highly successful outcomes – and, in some cases, with the humbling results and accompanying sense of failure that teaches the best learned lessons.

Our education has been enhanced by serving as directors on the boards of SMEs and global companies in a diverse range of sectors: food, engineering, utilities, textiles, life sciences, transport, financial services and general manufacturing.

The experience we have gathered over the years includes consulting assignments on business growth, exporting, selling, entrepreneurship, corporate governance and leadership, with hundreds of SMEs and large corporations.

In addition to learning from the irreplaceable lessons of life, we are avid readers of current business literature and are regular learning participants at cutting-edge institutions such as the Harvard Business School, IMD and Henley.

Reflecting on this direct and indirect contact with businesses large and small, our main conclusion is that effective leadership is by far the most important determinant in the successful growth of a company. Associated with this is our observation that SMEs led by leaders who practise the behaviours of STAR leadership in the main will deliver stellar growth.

Our motivation in writing this book is that the bulk of leadership business literature, whether academically-based or populist, appears either to be directed, at one extreme, to the leadership of very large enterprises or, at the other, to be focused on how individual entrepreneurial performance can be enhanced.

While such books do contain universal truths, their relevance to the role of leadership in small or medium-sized enterprises is largely overlooked. In our real-life experience, this is a serious omission, as the operating realities of a very large corporation with its deep support systems are dramatically different from those of a relatively resource-starved entrepreneurial company.

A DAY IN THE LIFE – SME LEADER, MIKE SULLIVAN, 6 NOVEMBER 2007

Mike Sullivan, MD of 45-employee SME Heritage Furniture, leaves home at 7am for his half-hour drive to the factory and, within minutes, is on the phone to the early shift foreman to check whether yesterday's delayed production run is back on track.

He is nervous, because the buyer from his top customer is due to call at 9am to follow through on her angry discussion with him the previous day, when he asked for a 24-hour extension on her cancellation deadline.

Mike is also stressed because he has a difficult meeting to face at 7.45, when he has to give his brother-in-law, the company sales manager, who has done an outstanding job in filling the firm's order book, a final warning about his repeated bullying of staff.

After 20 rings, the phone at the factory is finally answered. He is given the news that there has been an overnight machinery breakdown and no progress has been made with the delayed order. It is now 7.20am. Mike makes a snap decision to turn his car and make the 90-minute drive to the customer's head office, so as to arrive there before she phones him. His prompt action defuses the situation and he gets to Heritage at 11.30, by which time his brother-in-law has left on a weeklong sales trip.

Waiting for him in reception are two angry people: his main timber supplier, demanding immediate payment before any further deliveries will be made, and the environmental inspector, who is investigating a toxic leakage into the adjoining waterway.

Both are temporarily mollified by the promise of meetings on the following morning, which Mike had planned to take as a half-day holiday to go with his wife to the Open Day at his son's school.

He and the company accountant spend the next two hours planning the cash flow and worrying about how they will break the news to the bank that Heritage will exceed its facility again. Ironically, this is due to the good news that sales are growing rapidly and thus consuming more and more working capital.

It is now 4.30pm. Mike grabs a slightly stale sandwich and heads for the factory floor to help the fitter get the production line back up to speed.

The work drags on. Finally, they get it fixed and he leaves to go home at 7.15pm. His family are very disappointed and displeased that he will miss the school Open Day – and he still has to prepare for those dreaded meetings in the morning … .

A DAY IN THE LIFE – LARGECO LEADER, SEAN MACKLE, 6 NOVEMBER 2007

Sean Mackle is CEO of Irish-based Blix Pharma, a 1,600-employee subsidiary of Blix Global Life Sciences of Atlanta, Georgia.

At 7am, he is collected by his driver for the one-hour drive to Dublin and a breakfast presentation to analysts with his vice-president of finance and the chairman of Blix Pharma. Sitting in the comfortable back seat of the company Lexus limousine, he reviews his PowerPoint slides and, once again, carefully rehearses his speech.

At breakfast, the atmosphere is cordial and, though the analysts' questions are incisive and challenging, he and his team are well-prepared and answer confidently and capably.

Sean and the chairman then go to a conference room in the Merrion Hotel, where they spend two hours discussing the agenda for the monthly board meeting. Next is lunch in the hotel's Michelin two-starred restaurant with the company's corporate finance advisors, over which they consider the various financial instruments available to fund the new plant extension.

After lunch, Sean returns to Blix Pharma HQ for the regular mid-week management meeting with his Executive Leadership Team. This discussion finishes sharp at 5pm, having produced a list of actions for the ELT, covering both operational problems and planning for emerging opportunities.

Sean arrives home at 6pm, changes into formal attire and leaves for Dublin to host a table at the IBEC dinner, where his special guest is the US ambassador. As he enjoys the wine and the company, he fleetingly feels a sense of concern as he anticipates the next day's afternoon meeting with the trade unions. The discussions are likely to be very contentious.

But he smiles as he thinks of the pleasant morning he will have before the union meeting, when he attends the school Open Day with his wife and daughter … .

ONE DAY – TWO LIVES

We don't suggest that the cameos above are 'typical' days, but they are both based on real-life experiences. The main point in their telling is to illustrate the stark behavioural differences and contrasts in dynamics between leading a rapidly-growing SME and leading a large successful corporation.

A key conclusion from this comparison of two intelligent hard-working CEOs is that their training and development needs are strikingly different, and that the bulk of leadership business literature and leadership development courses are designed with Sean Mackle in mind. Sean's corporation will be delighted to send him to Harvard Business School or IMD for two weeks a year and to involve him in corporate retreats on a regular basis. He has the deep support team in place to allow this to happen.

It is different for Mike Sullivan. Ironically, he is the individual, who with his top team, could gain the greater benefit from appropriate reading and training. The biggest problem in bringing help to Mike is that, due to his relatively chaotic work patterns, he has very little time available to dedicate to his own improvement or that of his team.

The good news for Mike – and for you, if you are in a similar situation – is that this problem can be greatly eased if Mike – or you – really want to make it happen. We repeatedly speak to leaders who say that their situation is unique and that they can't change the pattern of their lives at work. No, it is not unique and, yes, it can be changed if you force it to happen.

The answer, as we have observed in many companies, lies first in training and empowering your team, to the point where the individuals are capable of taking greater responsibility, thus releasing more of your own time. Then, you must discipline yourself to use that additional freedom in self-development, rather than filling the vacuum with more activity.

Not easy, but it definitely can be done. This book is written for leaders like you and Mike Sullivan.

Noel Tichy and Warren Bennis are probably the modern era's two most influential and respected writers on leadership. Their article, 'Making judgement calls – the ultimate act of leadership',[1] forcibly makes our point:

> When Best Buy CEO Brad Anderson made the judgement in 2002 that his company needed to be transformed into a customer-centric enterprise, he began a process that would take years of focus and effort. In fact, he didn't make the final call until a team of executives had spent a couple of months exploring potential customer segments – the preparation phase.
>
> Then, once he had made the call, he mobilised six senior level task forces to spend six months choosing the first segments the company should cultivate.

---

[1]   *Harvard Business Review*, October 2007.

Team of executives! Couple of months! Six senior-level task forces! Six months! Try telling that by way of counselling guidance on making a judgement call to Mike Sullivan, or a cash-strapped lonely owner of a 15-person SME in Coleraine, Carlow, Cardiff, Cumbernauld or Carlisle.

So the CEO, board and top team try to take guidance from business literature that ignores the dynamics of running a relatively small business. In the main, they are limited in their opportunities to learn at top business school courses because, even if the content was tailored to the needs of an SME, they simply cannot afford to be away from their day-to-day responsibilities for the required time.

From our widespread experience of ownership and consulting, we also conclude that the essence of business success through effective leadership is relatively simple to understand. We take our cue on simplicity from Warren Buffett:

> *The business schools reward difficult complex behaviour more than simple behaviour, but simple behaviour is more effective.*

Yet commonsense approaches to the implementation of effective leadership often are ignored in the futile search for 'silver bullet' complex solutions, or are overwhelmed by the waves of detail involved in growing a company.

THE STAR MODEL

From our consulting interventions with leaders and executive top teams in SMEs, we have created a simple, real-life-based model that clearly articulates leadership – in terms of vision, team-building, selling, managing and innovation – around the goal of stellar growth. It describes best-practice approaches using real-life examples and demonstrates how you can measure your own competence across a range of 120 critical behaviours.

We freely acknowledge that the identification of the critical behaviours in the STAR model owes more to common-sense observations of "what works" in real-life, rather than to academic rigour. However, their validity has been tested over time in hundreds of consulting assignments.

The authentic stories we tell of real SME leaders in Ireland, Britain and the United States, dealing with real-life challenges, will guide you from their experiences, to change for the better the path of your own business.

We don't use theatrically-enhanced heroic tales, though many of the examples we quote describe the work of true heroes. We do not go into lengthy scene-setting or detailed description of unfolding events. Nor do we create fictional dialogue to colour the narrative. These are all real people, real names, real companies.

Nonetheless, as trusted advisors and confidants, we respect and guard the privacy of our clients. Hence, where there is sensitive or confidential information in the case examples – there are only a few such – the names of companies and individuals have been disguised, without losing the impact of the specific point being made.

Our aim here is to tell stories with which you can empathise and identify, so that your imagination moves you to create your own new story containing valuable lessons, applicable within the context of your own business.

From personal experience, we know that running an SME can be a perilous undertaking and that, in addition to its sometime rewards, it can result in horrendous worry for the risk-taking entrepreneur. Having experienced both states at various times, and having made our share of mistakes, we hesitate to offer advice, although there is a good deal of 'how to' contained in this book.

This book is written specifically for executive managers, directors, CEOs and non-executive directors of the SME companies that employ 56% of the people in the UK and Ireland and represent 99% of the businesses in these islands.

We hope our stories from the front-line of SME endeavour will deserve the 'truth well told' descriptor we borrow from the McCann-Erickson advertising agency's slogan but, much more, we want them to help you towards personal and corporate success on your STAR leadership journey.

1
SME LEADERSHIP

BASIC LEADERSHIP & OWNERSHIP

Most micro-businesses can operate quite successfully without formal disciplines. They expand to the SME state, bringing positive attributes, such as speed and flexibility, but also carrying negatives, such as lack of reporting discipline and organisational operating weakness.

Over the years, we have observed a strong correlation between the formal clarity with which an SME is structured and its subsequent attainment of stellar goals. The earlier such structuring can take place the better: preferably as soon as a micro-business morphs into an SME – the arrival of new investment and external influence is often the trigger for this positive step.

An SME with a formally-established top team, carrying clear responsibility and role accountability to its leader, has a crucial contribution to make to the initial establishment of challenging visionary goals. Their involvement in goal-setting brings the benefit that their commitment to delivery, as individuals and as a team, will be bought-in from day one.

Many SMEs operate without a functioning board of directors to whom the STAR leader can report and thus they suffer the consequences of this weakness, by delivering sub-optimal performance. Experienced leaders and non-executive directors ensure that this cornerstone of business structure is established and operating effectively.

The typical share register in a micro-business is simple indeed. Normally, the promoter is the sole shareholder, perhaps with the support of a partner or other family member. Ill-judged decisions on share allocation and cash-raising in the early days of transition can return later to haunt the promoter and, at worst, can taint the ownership structure with terminal pathological weakness.

We have worked with companies, where, in the early days when the shares were worth next-to-nothing, they were sold for next-to-nothing. But more significantly, they were sold to individuals who were not aligned to the goals of the promoter in the long-term. Little thought was given to the long-term; the only objective was to raise short-term cash.

As an SME leader with STAR leadership potential and with stellar dreams, you should never bring investors onto the share register just to raise money. You need them to bring something more than just the cash: they must have a long-term contribution to make to your ambitious, growing company.

Remember, minority shareholders have strongly entrenched rights in company law. Thus, extending the ownership of a company should never be taken lightly, nor new names added to the share register without serious thought.

Business angel, or venture capital, investment, can fill the funding gap and, while anecdotally, it is often described as 'expensive money', in most cases the reality is that such investment is the best thing that could happen to an early-stage SME. Experienced angels or VCs bring the money for growth, but they also bring contacts, expertise, experience, discipline and commitment to your aggressive, stellar-growth plan.

For over 10 years, our Amtec Medical and Linkubator companies have known and worked with Northern Ireland-based VC investor Crescent Capital. The value delivered to growing SMEs by Crescent's highly-professional investing team is seen clearly in their support for several stellar-growth companies, including Andor Technology, Lagan Technologies and APT.

Andor was a spin-out company from Queen's University. While the technical competence of its leaders and the technological competitive advantage carried by its intellectual property promised great things for the future, Andor's stellar growth was copper-fastened by the decision to bring Crescent on board as a VC investor. The involvement of an investment partner encouraged Andor to strengthen the management team, engage in personal learning and avail of advice from Crescent as Andor underwent periods of challenge to a successful IPO in December 2004.

LEADERSHIP TYPES

The single entrepreneur

Some leaders of SMEs begin their journey as founding entrepreneurs with no previous experience in running a business, let alone in managing or leading other people. However, they may have positive foundational skills:

- Highly-developed self-leadership.
- Technical or professional proficiency.
- The ability to build relationships to advance their objectives.
- Time management and punctuality.
- Reliability.
- The drive to succeed.

The conscious leadership ability to achieve objectives through the efforts of others, and the self-confidence to trust someone to deliver results, mark the beginning of real growth in an SME micro-business.

The early-stage SME leader

With faster growth and an increasing team, the theory goes that a leader has more leverage with which to continue the onward and upward progress, but rarely does this happen in practice. In the real world, the onward and upward progress is achieved, often because the leader works harder and harder, while missing the opportunity to bring out the best in the workforce.

The informal top team

As the SME continues to expand successfully, growth pressures force the leader and his managers to organise, plan and prioritise in perhaps a fairly haphazard fashion, but one that enables a relatively informal structure to re-actively apply some of the positive characteristics of leadership. However, significantly, there is no board leadership, because there is no board, and true strategic direction is absent.

Natural leaders emerge at different levels to cope with changing situations within the SME and perform with good effect. Often the titular leader, who relentlessly drove the early growth, finds it difficult to make the next transition to the stage where he effectively leads, and keeps, the managers who report directly to him.

The absence of a well-functioning board results in a lack of strategic direction, there is little real accountability and formal corporate governance is non-existent. Recurring crises ensure that the overall performance of the SME will plateau, at best, and may even suffer serious decline.

The SME leader needs a robust corporate structure and the essential skills of effective delegation, change management, coaching and emotional intelligence. He must enable the establishment of a board of directors, see that there are regular well-run board meetings and oversee effective implementation of the next leadership transition. Otherwise, without the ability to cascade leadership expertise to his direct reports, the exciting growth ride of the past few years is all but over.

The professional top team

The importance of the role of the board of directors cannot be over-stated. In the words of Bob Garratt,[2] 'the fish rots from the head', so the board and its chairman must perform well for the SME to prosper. The board must deliver its board goals, as well as supporting the CEO leader in pursuit of the enterprise goals.

Noel Tichy writes about the importance of leadership to the performance of huge multi-national corporations, although his comments are equally applicable to an SME. The core of his

[2] Bob Garratt, *The Fish Rots from the Head: The Crisis in Our Boardrooms - Developing the Crucial Skills of the Competent Director*, HarperCollins Business, 1997.

message is that the meaning of true leadership is contained in the phrase 'everyone a leader'. Every employee can take the personal entrepreneurial responsibility to be a leader of their own area, however lowly in the organisation, however humble.

It is the duty of the leader of an SME to ensure that Tichy's mantra is embedded within the soul of the organisation. The achievement of this key objective demands time, commitment, understanding, vision and tailored training. The standard 'sheep dip' approach to people development, where everyone is put through the same process, simply does not work.

Evaluation, customisation and skilled teaching are essential elements in the embedding of leadership for competitive advantage, and sufficient time must be dedicated to acquiring the skills and employing the behaviours.

The family group

The classic source of funding for business start-ups is promoter's cash, supplemented by investment from family and friends. It is no surprise, therefore, that the vast majority of SMEs are owner-managed and are often described as 'family businesses'. The term has no more substance or standing in civil or corporate law than, for example, 'lifestyle businesses', yet there are significant dynamics at work that justify a closer look at the family business in the context of SME leadership.

Some of these dynamics are extremely positive; however, many are destructively toxic and are the source of much of the consulting work we do for SMEs. The following is a true story, typical of many family business situations.

K ennedy Manufacturing celebrated 30 years in business last year with a party for staff, leading customers and suppliers and, of course, the extended family of the 80-year-old chairman and main shareholder, Fred Kennedy.

This is a profitable firm and, while it has provided a good living to the family for many years, it is now in extreme danger of following the fate of thousands of SMEs which, despite a good start under the charismatic leadership of the founder, fail to survive the generational transition.

Kennedy Manufacturing has a board of directors, chaired in name only by Fred, who has been retired for the past 15 years but occasionally sits in on management meetings. There is no STAR leader.

His son Henry is MD and another son, two daughters and their husbands comprise the rest of the board and also have executive roles in the business. They obviously have a high level of contact, both in day-to-day work and socially within the family.

The board never meets formally and, according to Henry:

> "… *strategic decisions are taken at management meetings, though it is hard to make them stick*".

All the direct family members are minority shareholders and the lack of formal corporate governance and coherent leadership spells potential doom for this formerly-strong SME.

The challenge is severe, because the family is divided and riven with political intrigue, all of which adds nothing to the future well-being of the commercial enterprise. An added complication is that, in common with many of the family businesses with which we have worked, the root of much of the dissension lies in envy, not between members of the direct family, but between their spouses.

The resolution of this perilous situation will require a monumental shift in thinking, to overcome not only the structural weaknesses deeply embedded in the firm, but also to deal with the powerful emotional factors that drive both family connectivity and sibling rivalry.

Then, when a formal professional structure is in place, realistically still mainly populated by Kennedy family members, the leadership must be strong and resolute in following a clear strategic vision to ensure the future prosperity of the company and, indeed, the extended Kennedy family. The jury is still out as to whether a STAR leader will emerge to lead Kennedy Manufacturing into a stellar-growth era.

ENTERPRISE GOALS

Clear definition of goals is a vital element in the achievement model for any individual or organisation. It is significant to note how the levels of aspiration towards set goals, while completely intangible in themselves, can affect achievement outcomes directly. To borrow from Michelangelo:

> *The tragedy for most of us is not that we aim too high and miss it, but that we aim too low and hit it.*

We classify Michelangelo's high aspirational goals as 'rich goals', to distinguish them from the important, though lesser, operational goals of an SME.

Where stellar growth is demanded by the board of an SME, the CEO, through confident inspirational leadership, must turn aspiration into clear measurable goals, must obtain commitment by the top team and must communicate the challenging agenda throughout the firm.

It is critical that the board and CEO take careful note of the wider world when setting ambitious aspirational targets. Obviously, the relevant market size and its rate of growth is important, but of greater importance is the overall competitive landscape. Michael Porter's original thinking on competitive strategy[3] has stood the test of time. Perhaps uniquely among theories in the vast number of business books published in recent years, his incisive model on the forces driving competition in an industry can be applied as effectively to goal-setting in the smallest micro-SME as in the largest multi-national enterprise.

---

[3]   Michael E. Porter, *Competitive Advantage: Creating & Sustaining Superior Performance*, The Free Press, 1985.

GROWTH BARRIERS

The SME leadership task has only just begun with the setting of challenging 'rich goals' and development of a coherent business plan. Then the list of obstacles is added to by competitive pressures, external factors, internal problems and sheer mental stress. But bad luck, fear of failure and loneliness arguably are the most difficult barriers with which the SME leader has to cope on the journey to stellar growth.

Bad luck

Amtec Medical, a medical devices SME we have owned for some years, provides an example of the impact of the luck factor. In 2001, its previous momentum of stellar growth suffered the shock of hitting a 'sheer bad luck' barrier that almost killed the business. Thankfully, after several years of hard work and good leadership by the team, the catastrophic setback has been overcome and growth resumed – but here is the story.

A mtec had acquired the world rights to an exciting disruptive medical technology and had invested heavily in developing the early prototypes and in negotiating with global corporations that had the distributive muscle to ensure delivery of the product to worldwide markets.

One of these global giants, Mallinckrodt of St Louis, USA, entered into protracted discussions and investigations with Amtec, which culminated in a 200-page draft contract for Mallinckrodt to obtain the worldwide distribution rights for the product and, in return, to acquire 10% of Amtec's ordinary equity by an investment of £4 million. This valued our small Irish SME at £40 million.

Now for the sheer bad luck barrier: the due diligence process was under way and proceeding without a hitch, when right out of the blue the $4 billion Mallinckrodt was bought by Tyco, at that time in the full flush of its Dennis Koslowsky acquisitive feeding frenzy.

Within a week, the Mallinckrodt team with whom we had been negotiating in St Louis, Boston, and Cologne, including the President, Vice-President of Strategic Acquisitions and Vice

President of European Operations, had been binned, along with hundreds of their colleagues. We had nobody to talk to and our contract finished up in the same bin.

This was a massive hit and Amtec was severely knocked back. From stellar growth to panic survival mode overnight. From STAR leadership to the ultimate test of our top team leadership skills. Amtec wobbled, struggled and survived against all the odds.

Thankfully, most barriers to stellar growth are not so dramatically sudden in their impact as sheer bad luck, though their debilitating effects demand entrepreneurial STAR leadership to ensure that they do not destroy the dreams, or stop the SME from achieving its rich goals.

The less cataclysmic barriers to stellar growth that challenge the leadership competences of SME leaders include:

- Getting sales.
- A lack of capital.
- Hiring good managers.
- Building top teams.
- Getting – and keeping – good employees.
- Getting rid of bad employees.
- A lack of new ideas.
- A lack of ambition.
- Not choosing rich goals.

All of the above can impede progress towards achievement of full potential for an SME, but there is a barrier factor missing from that list, which is present to some degree with the leader of every growth-oriented company of whatever size or category. It can be the greatest barrier of all – the fear of failure.

Fear of failure

If you can meet with Triumph and Disaster, and treat those two impostors just the same … .

Rudyard Kipling's words carry a powerful message for SME leaders.

The lesson for our moments of success is that we should not get too carried away with our own alleged brilliance and, for our incidents of failure, that we should not be too downcast. The frequent humbling results from hubris will deal with the former state, but it often takes a conscious positive pro-activity to deal with the latter. SME leaders need to fight the fear of failure.

Having suffered our own dark nights of the soul and consulted with numerous under-pressure executives, we firmly believe that the ability to fight the fear of failure is a country's, a company's and a person's fundamental component of competitive advantage. To help in fighting this insidious fear, the leader should always remember that failure is an incident and not an identity.

Many people seem to take a delight in attaching the label of failure to business people, either from plain envy of earlier successes, or for commercial advantage.

I n 2002, after the Mallinckrodt incident in Amtec, the company badly needed to raise cash. So we tramped around the venture capital funders in Dublin and the City of London, with our presentation on the future of the business.

In one memorable presentation to a group of four high-powered people in the City, John was receiving the customary grilling and was holding his own, in the face of incisive, but unnecessarily hostile, questioning. The situation was intimidating enough without this aggressive tone. We were on the 16th floor of some of the most expensive real-estate in London, sitting in an oak-panelled boardroom at a massive table under crystal chandeliers.

The public school, Harvard Business School-educated venture capitalist, whom we will call Henry, pried and probed in, frankly, a very condescending way, but still John answered courteously and capably to every question – except what proved to be the last.

> *"I recognise that your company has a strong IP position and the financial prospects look good. So good that we feel comfortable in looking at making an investment. But you failed to complete your Mallinckrodt deal, so I have to ask myself 'Why I should invest in failures like you people?'."*

John jumped to his feet, threw the pencil he was holding at Henry and, with passion, told him that, yes, we had failed with Mallinckrodt, yes, we had failed at many things and yes, we would fail at many things in the future, but he was not going to sit there and let us be called failures.

We didn't get the investment.

On the way down in the mirrored elevator, Will assured John that he agreed with every word he had uttered and that he should never allow anyone to call him a failure, but:

"Son, you shouldn't have thrown the pencil at Henry".

John looked his father in the eye and spat out:

"Will, I wish it had been a brick!".

We failed to get Henry's money, but we roared with laughter – and we were certainly not failures. Failure is an incident, not an identity.

The crucially important fact, of which leaders must constantly remind themselves, is that failure is the catalytic spark at the heart of all wealth creation. It is the essential link in the entrepreneurial causal chain. Failure must occur.

If there is no failure, there is no risk; if there is no risk, there is no entrepreneurship; if there is no entrepreneurship, there is no added value; if there is no added value, there is no wealth creation; if there is no wealth creation, there is no business; if there is no business, there is no prosperity – for anyone.

Failure must occur. So we encourage leaders to fight the fear – and cope, reminding themselves of the compensations of leading a value-adding enterprise. To paraphrase Ralph Bauer, who led his Thomas Ferguson Irish linen company through turbulent high-risk change, as the industry suffered dramatic contraction in the late 20th century:

If you want a comfortable risk-free life, if you want security, if you want repetition, do not consider leading a company. If however, you want to make things, to contribute to economic wellbeing by aiding the creation of wealth, then come into business; to be challenged, to be stimulated, to innovate, to risk-take, to develop, to have excitement and to have fun.

Leadership loneliness

The STAR leader of a stellar-growth SME must demonstrate competence and control in the face of difficulty and barriers to growth. Often, in addition, he has to deal with an insidious debilitating internal factor, accentuated by its invisibility to colleagues and the outside world: the 'black dog' of loneliness.

This issue has significant importance in the stellar-growth SME and is seldom addressed; we will tell you about it in the light of an incident in our experience – a true story:

I n 2003, as the main speaker at a major business conference, Will, with the rest of the enthralled audience, listened to Owen Robinson tell the story of how he started work as a humble apprentice fitter in the machine shop of a textile mill.

With passion, Owen told how he was made redundant in the collapse of textile manufacturing in the late 1970s, started his own one-man business and built it into a £15 million enterprise. He proudly related how, from his lowly beginnings, he now lived in a Georgian mansion and was driven in a chauffeured limousine.

His riveting speech was delivered with confident, self-deprecating humour and hilarious, well-told anecdotes. Owen inspired the entire audience and deservedly received a standing ovation.

Will's subject at the conference was 'How to lead a growing company'. In an introductory aside to his address, and based on his own personal experience of leading a stellar-growth SME, he referred briefly to the issue of loneliness:

> "I am speaking to an audience of highly successful company leaders and, as I look down from this podium, I see confident, prosperous executives. I saw many of you drive into the car park of this convention centre in your Mercedes, or Bentley, or Maserati, displaying the fruits of your success in leading the accelerating growth of your business – and you deserve every bit of it.
>
> I see achievement, which has taken your small businesses from obscurity to market positions that are the envy of your competitors; and you are still growing aggressively for the future.
>
> But, because I have been there, I also know there can be a dark, dark, secret side to your façade of success. I have felt the fear myself and I

know that, behind the face the public sees, many of you are tortured and twisted by loneliness.

Despite all your social and business contacts, you really have nobody to talk to who shares your deepest fears and most intractable problems. You are crippled with loneliness and the fear of failure.

As the great Antarctic explorer, Ernest Shackleton, put it, 'Leadership is a fine thing, but it has its penalties. And the greatest penalty is loneliness'".

That was all, and then Will got on with the rest of his speech.

After the event, as he walked to his car, Will saw Owen Robinson approaching, nervous, agitated and drawing heavily on a cigarette. He was far from the confident personality of two hours ago and struggled to speak:

"Will, when you talked about loneliness, you were speaking only to me. Everybody thinks I'm a great success, but I'm an empty shell. Yes, my business is great; yes, I can put on a great show, but I am as frightened as a little kid, because I'm alone and I have nobody who can listen and help me with some awful problems, which threaten my company. It feels like I am being attacked personally, and I have no defence, and nobody to turn to for help. You are the first person I have ever heard who has admitted publicly to the same problem. Will you help me?"

Owen's problems were rooted in minority shareholder dissension and the matter was seriously compromised, in that some of his bitterest opponents were family members, who were threatening him with pressure that came very close to out-and-out blackmail. The complexity of the problems, together with the powerful emotional overlay, left Owen mentally paralysed and unable to cope with finding a solution.

Will acted as a coach to him over the next three years, during which time Owen courageously faced and solved his issues. Getting rid of his problems, and the associated demons of his mind, freed Owen to focus on accelerating the stellar expansion of his company, through organic growth and a strategic acquisition, which has taken the Robinson enterprise to a turnover in excess of £50 million.

OUR SEARCH FOR A LEADERSHIP MODEL

SMEs can succeed or fail in the short term for many reasons but, in both eventualities, we have observed an interesting dysfunction between the success or failure of the company and that of the leadership. It is demonstrably not always the case that good leadership correlates with successful business, or that bad leadership matches with failure. It is beyond dispute, however, that the chances of positive outcomes are greatly increased by good leadership.

The important factors in judging quality of leadership, whether in a business going well or one failing, are:

- Fit for purpose.
- Balance.

The obvious need to make the judgement on these grounds, rather than the business' performance, is that changing a good leadership team in a bad business will not, of itself, make the business better. As Warren Buffett puts it:

> *When a management team with a reputation for brilliance tackles a business with a reputation for bad economics, it is the reputation of the business that remains intact.*

Assuming the individual or team in place is fit for purpose, in terms of technical and management competence, the key determinant as to whether the business will be optimised for good or ill lies with the balance of leadership skills in the individual leader, or in the leadership top team. A highly-motivated individual entrepreneur certainly can take things quite a long way and can achieve a creditable level of success – up to a point.

The initial excitement of starting a business, entering a new market, launching a new product or gaining a first major customer is a powerful motivator. Such excitement can inspire super-human performance and superior differentiating customer service to early customers. This is entrepreneurial selling and leadership in practice, delivering customer-centric service beyond the company's known resources, but it is difficult, if not impossible, for an individual to sustain such a level of attention over time, as the company expands.

Stellar growth is the measure of success for a leadership team: growth in profits, growth in turnover, growth in market reach, growth in status. Early excitement and initial customer-centric focus can lose their force in a rapid growth situation, if there is an inability to change the total organisation in line with the demands of its expansion.

Remember and reflect on Charles Darwin's piercing message in the context of evolutionary development:

> *It's not the strongest, nor the most intelligent, that survives – it's the one most adaptable to change.*

With growth, SME leaders encounter change and change demands adaptation, so that customers remain central, in order to deliver sustainable sales increases.

The magic of entrepreneurial selling can run out as a company becomes more rigid, as time is devoted and diverted to non-selling areas – and, if there is no process model or road-map to guide the leader, confusion, despair and weariness can result.

Most new ventures, whether start-up or within a developing larger SME, fail for the simple reason that they do not hit their sales numbers. As John King, one of the most successful leaders in Irish business, bluntly says:

> *… at the end of the day, the only thing that really matters in business is sales.*

Sales revenue is the life blood of the company and, in a sole promoter start-up, or development situation, responsibility for the sales starts and ends with one lonely person. There are no key account managers, there are no sales people on the road, there are no marketing experts and there is little process.

Whether this lonely leader's strength is as a visionary, team-builder, innovator, manager, or an experienced seller, the need to get sales is vital. In essence, this one person is the entire sales and marketing team. She must cover all the requirements of establishing the business, bringing in the funding, arranging for production, supervising manufacturing, and all the other myriad tasks, while at the same time being an effective seller.

For a short spell of time, she can do it, but for a limited number of initial customers only – and these customers do experience the full power of her entrepreneurial selling. However, this is a tough agenda for any time, and any team, let alone a micro enterprise. It's often a nightmare for the start-up leader but she still gets it done, just about – so long as the business stays small.

It's when she grows the business, and the inevitable requirements for change come along, that she hits big trouble. Trouble that needs answers and help in creating and leading the balanced team that has the firepower to deliver stellar-growth.

All our business consulting experience, exposure to academic literature and comprehensive research, tells us that successful high-growth enterprises are created, developed and sustained by STAR leaders leading high-performance entrepreneurial leadership teams. We developed the STAR leadership model by identifying the leadership behaviours required for stellar SME growth.

Many venture capitalists are on record as saying that they do not back bright ideas, attractive market sectors, glossy business plans or persuasive business models. The fundamental touchstone of their decision-making is that they back competent, ambitious, well-balanced and well-led teams.

This is great in an ideal world, but the world of the SME leader is seldom perfect, and that idealised well-balanced team may not be there just when it is needed. Further, even when the leader is fully aware that she needs immediate help to cope with growth, she's sometimes not quite sure where she needs it, what type of help she needs, or where it can be found. Often, she is not even able to clearly articulate what she needs.

This is where the STAR model is of great help to the leader, in guiding a process of evaluation to create a balanced leadership team, fit for purpose in the SME's environment.

The model is a simple, understandable representation of a complex dynamic activity; a guiding framework comprising five vital balancing process attributes, all focussed on the centricity of the company goals:

- Vision.
- Team-building.
- Selling.
- Managing.
- Innovation.

True entrepreneurs know that labelling entrepreneurial leadership as a 'process' demands caution. In addition to its sometime routine drudgery, entrepreneurial leadership can be intuitive, instinctive, re-actionary, pro-active, exciting, terrifying, sometimes irrational, and frequently chaotic – anything but process.

But, if the precious magic leadership dynamic of the entrepreneurial leader, which can deliver such positive sales growth results in early start-up days, can be 'bottled', or processed and clearly understood, it will be worth a fortune in successfully achieved goals. It will deliver success for the STAR leader / entrepreneur, the top team, the employees and the SME.

As the SME grows, the leader quickly finds it impossible to perform all of the tasks and requirements, even those at which she is very good and from which she derives great personal satisfaction. So she starts to hire and to delegate in hope. Unfortunately, the precious magic is often lost in the delegation. The well-intentioned efforts of her informal emergent team and the input of her own strengths, whether visionary, team-building, selling, managing, or innovating, can be significantly diluted in terms of their effect. If only the total team of which she is now a part could retain the 'bottled' magic and apply it, the future growth of the SME would be assured.

The broad object of this book and our leadership model is to help leaders apply this 'magic'. We understand the key behaviours by drawing on our own experiences and knowledge of hundreds of visionary, team-building, selling, managing, innovating and wild-card leader / entrepreneurs with whom we have worked.

The main purpose is to demonstrate how STAR leadership behaviours can deliver competitive advantage to fast-growth SME businesses in their pursuit of stellar goals.

STELLAR SME GROWTH

It is a truism that, if a business is not growing, it is in decline. As a result, it is rare to find an enterprise of any size that does not have to a greater or lesser degree the ambition to grow. Over their lifetime, some SMEs satisfy that aspiration by achieving a modest incremental growth; some that perhaps experienced rapid early expansion have settled into the mode of operation described as 'lifestyle businesses'; only a minority will achieve stellar growth.

The common factor that determines their rate of progress, regardless of the category into which they fall, is leadership: its capability, vision and sustained implementation. In our experience, the development of better leadership is the single lever that can accelerate business improvement more rapidly than any other and, if stellar-growth is the aim, then leadership is the vital key.

It is not difficult to get agreement that growth is good, and indeed good for all stakeholders in an enterprise. The SME itself becomes stronger, more profitable, better able to resist the competitive or cyclical pressures that could threaten its survival, and better able to reward its shareholders and employees financially.

The shareholders see their assets increase in value and they receive an above average rate of return on their investment.

The employees are aware that their employment is secure and, as they observe new hires coming on board, they take pride in being part of, and contributing to, the growth of a successful firm.

Growth brings great satisfaction to the managers, in that, as individuals, they have more direct reports, their jobs are expanded and there are ever-greater opportunities for promotion.

The visionary leaders see the ongoing realisation of their dreams and can enjoy the material and self-actualising rewards of achievement.

But growth, and in particular stellar growth, also has a dark side. In addition to its demonstrable benefits, it carries different levels of threat to all stakeholder constituencies. The rapidly-growing SME itself is exposed to change taking place in every aspect of its constitution and operations.

Provided the corporate structures are adjusted in line with these changes, in an analogous way to trimming the sails on a yacht, and provided correct leadership and management decisions are made on operations, then acceleration can continue successfully.

However, if the adjustment and management decisions are wrong or, which is quite common, they are neglected or abdicated, the results can be catastrophic. Stellar growth for the corporate entity carries a high, though manageable, degree of risk. Effective leadership, with robust corporate governance, is the antidote to this threat.

Obviously, any risk for the corporate SME has a contingent risk for the shareholders, whose investment established and subsequently sustains the enterprise. The shareholders have another threat to face. Stellar growth inevitably sucks in cash for increased working capital, new machinery, marketing and selling investment and added facilities. The shareholders are the direct, or indirect, first port of call for new funds.

These shareholders appoint the board and the board appoints the CEO, who leads the top team. Provided that this leadership can convince the shareholders of the soundness of their plans, the shareholders' threat is dealt with and the money will be forthcoming. Again, leadership is the key.

For the employees, the threats are mainly in the area of change and, while some people positively thrive on novelty, many react negatively to the associated disturbance to their routines. But, if an engaging vision is presented, and motivating leadership is employed effectively, then the fear of change can be turned into a motivational challenge and people will sacrifice the comfort of their routines, in order to participate in a common improvement for the firm, their colleagues and themselves. Leaders have a direct responsibility to communicate effectively and to bring the entire team with them, towards realisation of the vision.

The dark side of stellar growth for managers lies chiefly in the increasing burden of responsibility they have to bear and the hidden, though commensurately increased, need for them to develop their competence.

In a rapidly-growing SME, this is a real difficulty, as these managers simply do not have the time to attend all-day off-site training courses on a regular basis. The leadership input to deal with this threat is to ensure that in-house training and coaching is available, from the CEO and senior colleagues, supplemented by external expertise, where required.

2

SME LIFE–CYCLES

UNDERSTANDING CHANGE

The aware, competent, SME leadership team and its leader know that, however long a run of growth success may last, and however well they operate the internal affairs of the company, external business cycles can throw the best-laid plans into disarray. In addition, the experienced team knows that they need to pay careful attention to internal corporate life-cycle factors. In short, change in circumstances, whether internal or external, cannot be ignored.

Change creates new situations and, if these are to be optimised, in theory they demand new leaders; but, in the real world of pragmatism, it is simply not possible to renew the leadership so quickly – even though some large company boards may appear to make knee-jerk attempts at such a response, with rapid turnover of CEOs at each downward spike in the share price.

In the late 1960s, Ken Blanchard and Paul Hersey created a 'situational leadership' model,[4] which, despite, or maybe because of, its simplicity, has stood the test of time and examination through widespread application. It acknowledges the approach we all take in our dealings with the varied situations we find ourselves in as we live our daily lives, in that we adapt our behaviour and responses in the light of the situation.

Straightforward enough, but it is not unusual to observe leaders and their teams, who have been successful in one era, sector, or specific business, failing badly in a different set of circumstances;

---

[4]   Kenneth H. Blanchard & Paul Hersey, *Management of Organisational Behaviour*, Prentice-Hall.

perhaps because they have not altered their responses in an appropriate fashion, or because the behavioural traits that served them so well in the past are no longer appropriate.

Possibly one of the most powerful examples of this phenomenon is Sir Winston Churchill, Britain's outstanding leader throughout the crisis days of World War II. After coping with the enormous challenges of that threatening period, inspiring the Allied cause with a leader's rhetoric and ultimately delivering a victory, he found himself rejected by the people as leader for the new post-war world. His political leadership life-cycle had run its course.

The influence of life-cycles is real, not only for the individual, but also for SMEs, their products, markets, machinery, people, teams and material prosperity. Leaders must ensure that the inexorable, inevitable effects of life-cycle-induced change are met with a flexibility of attitude, together with diligence in business planning at all levels. And, indeed, with an element of humility, as T.S. Eliot wrote:

> *We shall not cease from exploration,*
> *And the end of all our exploring,*
> *Will be to arrive where we started*
> *And know the place for the first time.*

These lines capture the essence of human endeavour, with its cyclical process of curiosity, investigation, pursuit of novelty, ambition, desire and grand designs. Eliot's accurate perception, in a few words, cuts through the implicitly-stated permanence of our achievements, and reminds us of the remorseless, natural cyclicality of life.

Not that life-cycles are necessarily negative. Indeed, the highest levels of human and business satisfaction are reached when we truly 'know a place for the first time', accept its realities and react with a clearly understood positive response to the challenges, opportunities and threats of the situation.

This is analogous to living happily in a seasonal climate, by making adjustments in response to the cycle of Spring, Summer, Autumn and Winter. The key to living successfully and happily in an environment of seasonality is a positive acceptance of the inevitability of the cycle, and then a determination to prepare pro-actively for each of its phases.

Cyclicality is the natural, remorseless, inevitable order, whether applied to the changing seasons, our lives as individual human beings, or indeed the emergence, growth, maturity, decline and sometime rebirth and renewal of business enterprises.

Acceptance and analysis of this natural order, and the positive management of response to its predictable cyclical changes, does not deliver perfection; but it dramatically reduces the negative downsides of 'boom and bust' and supports the sustainability of an SME's relative business performance over time.

After many years of direct involvement in, and consulting to, companies of all sizes in fast-changing environments, we are convinced that a key positive influence on future business growth is based on a clear understanding of the dynamic cycles with which a corporation engages, both internal and external.

The cascade of business literature that followed the success of *In Search of Excellence*[5] in the early 1980s has spewed out theories, fads, and well-argued academic treatises on how to build the perpetually excellent company. *Built to Last*,[6] *Good to Great*,[7] and the many 'how to' entrepreneurial offerings, all suggest new wisdom that, if implemented, will ensure long-term success in business.

This torrent of advice, despite its frequently well-argued and helpful ideas and concepts, often misses much of the point, by its focus on the attainment of a perfect state that is rarely, if ever, apparent in the real world of SME business.

There, we see natural, remorseless and inevitable cycles bringing change: good times, OK times and bad times; cycles for which the 'sheep dip' remedies of empowerment, re-engineering, competitive

---

[5]   Thomas J. Peters & Robert H. Waterman, *In Search of Excellence: Lessons from America's Best-run Companies*, HarperBusiness, 1982.

[6]   James C. Collins & Jerry I. Porras, *Built to Last: Successful Habits of Visionary Companies*, HarperBusiness, 1997.

[7]   Jim Collins, *Good to Great*, RandomHouse Business Books, 2001.

strategy, or entrepreneurship, despite their academic neatness, short-term helpfulness and idealism, do not provide long-term answers.

THE OPERATING CYCLE

The simple seminal model for an understanding of cyclicality in the business world lies in the basic operating cycle for all commercial transactions, as shown in **Figure 1**.

Figure 1: The Fundamental Cyclical Model for Commercial Transactions

Imagine the world of your neighbourhood Tesco or Sainsbury's supermarket operator:

- **Anticipating** – driven by **visionary** leadership: First, they anticipate your needs as you go shopping for the household. You enter a brightly-lit, welcoming entrance with attractive displays and the ambiance convinces you that you are in the right place – and you feel ready to buy.

- **Structuring** – driven by **team-building** leadership: Next, the well-organised team is unobtrusively, but obviously, in place, and operating in the slick co-ordinated fashion that makes it easy for you to buy.

- **Relating** – driven by **selling** leadership: Then the greeter relates to you as an individual, with a warm smile and a pleasant word. All the staff throughout the store develop this relationship by being friendly and helpful – and you feel comfortable as a customer.

- **Executing** – driven by **managing** leadership: The vital fourth stage in the cycle is execution: products are visible, available, just what you want at the right price, and there are no queues at the check-out – you are having a positive experience.

- **Learning** – driven by **innovating** leadership: While you are in the supermarket, with each aisle that you visit, with each selection you make, data is collected, which is applied to the final learning stage of the cycle. The operation learns about your preferences, patterns of shopping, and the prices you are prepared to pay. Tesco, or Sainsbury's, then can apply this learning, by informing the anticipating stage, and starting the cycle all over again.

This is the fundamental cyclical model for all commercial transactions and interfaces.

THE CLASSIC BUSINESS LIFE–CYCLE

The basic operating and leadership cycles, and the other cycles, are interesting in themselves. But it is their alignment, or smooth meshing like gear-wheels, that delivers the power of understanding necessary for the effective running of SME organisations over time. To illustrate this, consider the changing dominant features of leadership that apply to the classic model of the business life-cycle (see **Figure 2**):

- At birth, when **innovation** is critical for leadership, learning is the part of the operating cycle (see **Figure 1**) in focus.
- At start-up, when **vision** is critical for leadership, anticipating is the part of the operating cycle in focus.
- At the early-growth stage, **team-building** and structuring are the respective key areas of focus.
- In the growth stage, between early and late growth, **selling** and relating are the key areas of focus.
- In later-growth, **management** and executing are in focus.
- Maturity requires new **innovation** and anticipating to kick-start a new cycle – or else, decline and death are inevitable.

Figure 2: How the Dominant Features of Leadership Change during the Business Life-cycle

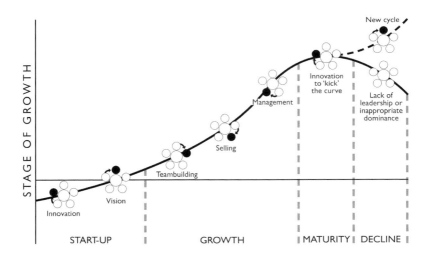

SME leaders are not helpless in the face of this remorseless cyclical reality. The well-led team will seek – and find – opportunity where others may struggle, through an acceptance, understanding, and pro-active approach to grasping the concept of business cyclicality.

Professor Albert Einstein, the Nobel Prize-winning physicist, in setting an examination for his graduate students as he did at the end of each academic year, handed the finished script to his secretary. She remarked, with surprised protest, that the questions he had set were identical to those set last year. To which, Einstein replied:

"Ah yes, but this year, the answers are different!".

Most business questions are familiar to us, but changing environments, markets and cycles ensure that the answers change, with a frustrating and challenging regularity.

The myopic view of much of the current business literature in presenting 'one-size-fits-all' formulaic answers is exposed in the research of Kim & Mauborgne,[8] where they assert that, over the past 100 years, there is not one perpetually high-performing company!

This is powerful support for our view that being aware of the effect of corporate life-cycles on an individual company and the leader's pro-active responses to predicted changes will bring greater long-term value than striving for an illusory perfection. Even if achieved, the perfect state will exist only for a moment in time, before its extinction, due to the remorseless advance of the cycles of change.

CHANGE & RESPONSE

The fundamentals are not about business skills, strategic insights, management 'how-to' or gung-ho inspiration, important as all these features may be. The fundamentals are about awareness of change and the understanding of complex business operations, through consideration of cyclical dynamics that are apparent in every company, SME, or multi-national.

Such perceptiveness will help SME leaders and managers to face realities, to deal with new situational dynamics and to cope

---

[8]   W. Chan Kim & Renée Mauborgne, *Blue Ocean Strategy: How to Create Uncontested Market Space & Make the Competition Irrelevant*, Harvard Business School Press, 2005.

optimally with success and growth. It will help them to acknowledge and face the inevitability of sclerotic encroachment and to anticipate, prepare for, and implement the actions required to halt and reverse its damaging effects. In other words, leaders and their teams will be equipped to deal with change.

Of course, change is not all about life-cycles, which by definition generally have a long-term context. The SME leader striving for stellar growth also has to contend with, and make decisions on, operational variables of all kinds in the course of each working day.

Decision-making for the leader and leadership team is initiated as a result of stimulus, intuition or judgement and, as there is seldom one right answer, the calls must be made on the basis of what seems the best way to make progress towards the company goals.

It is closely analogous to sailing a boat. The threat does not come from any single element, but from all the forces combining to produce complex variable changes, which demand controlled, firm responses. Just like leading a stellar-growth SME.

LIFE–CYCLES & SUSTAINABILITY

Ichak Adizes wrote a wonderful book,[9] analysing the corporate life cycle and arguing that leaders and managers should pursue a state of 'prime'. It is an idealistic and, in many ways, helpful approach to organisational design but, here in the real SME world, 'prime' does not appear to exist in any sustainable form.

Sustainability, or surviving over the long-term, never mind winning and achieving stellar-growth, requires that the SME leader reviews the evolutionary fitness of the company regularly.

From the dawn of mankind, individuals are driven by the search for evolutionary fitness and the ability to survive, so that our genes can contribute to the future of the species.

Harvard professors Paul Lawrence and Nitin Nohria suggest that there are four key drives, or questions, which define the

---

[9]   Ichak Adizes, *The Pursuit of Prime: Maximise Your Company's Success with the Adizes Program*, Knowledge Exchange, 1997.

human condition.[10] These four primary innate drivers, hard-wired in the brains of all individuals, which from earliest history have made people distinctly human, are:

- The drive to **learn**.
- The drive to **bond**.
- The drive to **acquire**.
- The drive to **defend**.

Lawrence & Nohria say:

> *Reflect a moment on your own life or the lives of others you are familiar with. We would predict that those who have found ways to satisfy all four drives (at least over time) will feel more fulfilled than those who have focused on some to the exclusion of others. Those who have neglected their drive to acquire are more likely to lack self-esteem and feel envious of those who have done better. Those who have neglected their drive to bond with others are apt to feel empty and disconnected from life. Those who have neglected their drive to learn and lived a life with little opportunity to pursue their own curiosities are more likely to feel stunted in their personal development. Those who have neglected their drive to defend or have been unable to do so are more likely to feel abused and victimized.*

> *Human beings are driven to seek ways to fulfil all four drives because these drives are the product of the species' common evolutionary fitness, that is, the ability of our genes to survive and carry on the species. The independence of these drives is what forces people to think and to choose – because **not all drives can be met at all times**. In short, the four drives are what make people distinctly human – complex beings with complex motives and complex choices.*

'Prime' cannot be sustained in the human life cycle, yet it is possible for most of us to live successful and satisfying lives while coping with cyclical vagaries, with some individuals enjoying truly stellar achievement. Much the same can be said for driven SMEs.

As with Einstein's exam, the questions remain fundamentally the same but, with constantly changing environments, threats,

---

[10]   Paul R. Lawrence & Nitin Nohria, *Driven: How Human Nature Shapes Our Choices*, Jossey Bass, 2001.

opportunities and challenges, the answers can assume a complexity so extreme as to defeat many and to be effectively responded to by only a few.

These few thrive through understanding the cycles, accepting their impact and creatively investing the appropriate drive or response to the relevant environmental cyclical challenge or opportunity. The STAR SME leader and their entrepreneurial company recognise and understand the dynamics of business cycles.

The 'strong' companies featured in one of the most famous business books of all time, *In Search of Excellence*, over the past 25 years since its publication, collectively have demonstrated serious weakness and, in many cases, even an inability to survive. Indeed, within two years of publication, *Business Week* reported that 14 of these 'best-run' companies in America had fallen on hard times.

Upstart, fast-moving, entrepreneurial enterprises intuitively understood the cyclical changes, grabbed the opportunities, and stole the markets of these formerly-powerful businesses. In many cases, these large companies had become complacent in their success, and failed to recognise and respond to the changes in their life-cycle. And, in due course, it's likely that some of the fast-growth SME upstarts also will be unable to cope with cyclical change.

Nokia of Finland is a clear example of how response to cyclicality can bring success, how its neglect brings failure, and how a re-focus on the new cycle can lead to recovery, allowing it to regain its foremost industry position.

I n an earlier era, Nokia was a successful, relatively small, low-technology, regional SME company manufacturing safety matches and rubber boots. It made a spectacular entrepreneurial change in shifting its focus to sophisticated high-technology product lines, in response to cyclical change. This was an unpredictable massive success, which ultimately turned Nokia from potential decline into a dominant global player in high-growth markets.

But, as one of the strongest of companies and the world leader in mobile phones, for a time Nokia's leaders resolutely refused to recognise major market changes, which were capitalised on by its smaller competitors. One of these changes of only a few years ago, to which Nokia turned a blind eye, was the need to design clamshell phones – the flip-open type still enjoying great popularity with customers. In Helsinki, in mid-2003, Nokia's executives were asked why the company was not designing phones to cater for this clear trend. The answer, as cited in the *Financial Times*, was a far cry from the spirit of the company's response to cycle-change of an earlier era, and betrayed its lack of understanding of the internal and external cycles affecting the business at that time.

Nokia's response was dismissive, almost contemptuous. Eero Miettinen, group design director, said the Finnish mobile giant had nothing against clamshells but that it wanted to offer some *"added value"*.

Anssi Vanjoki, an executive vice-president, sneeringly added that, to do that, Nokia's designers would have to come up with something more than *"… silver clamshell phones. I think we have to aim a little higher"*.

Nokia has paid a high price for its lofty disregard for customers' demands. In the last quarter of 2003, the company announced it had suffered a 2% fall in sales, despite buoyant growth in the market. It had led investors to expect its sales would grow at up to 7%. The company blamed a poor mix of phones, including lack of clamshells.

Ironically, one of the biggest winners from Nokia's discomfiture was Samsung, a South Korean company that did much to popularise the silver clamshells that Vanjoki dismissed. Richard Windsor, technology analyst at Nomura, estimates that Samsung has captured an additional 3% of the market – the percentage that Nokia lost, and more.

> *"Samsung is being more aggressive. The impact has been acute."*

But the problem goes beyond a single bad quarter. Nokia has been battling to defend its 40% share of the global mobile handset market at a time of technological change and against increasing competition from Asian manufacturers.

For Nokia, the world's biggest cell-phone maker, the questions of the time essentially were the same, but fashion-aware consumers demanded different, change-inducing answers. Despite its size, Nokia, or any other company, disregards such changes at its peril.

Indeed, Nokia listened and, by 2007, had fully recovered its position through aggressive innovation.

The Nokia case shows that the need for response to cyclical change is acutely relevant for the multi-national global player, just as it is to the small local start-up. This is validated by a quote from Jack Welch, when he ran the General Electric Corporation:

> *GE's goal is not to become smaller, but to get the small company soul and small company speed inside our big company body.*

The answer does not lie in strength, nor does it lie in superior intelligence. Seemingly counter-intuitively, there is well-documented evidence that entrepreneurial activity and business start-up levels are relatively low in countries with high attainment in secondary and post-secondary educational programmes.[11]

The tens of thousands of MBAs being produced world-wide each year have a weak track record in creating new SME business ventures or, when in management, of coping better with cyclical or market changes.

They want to be consultants. They want to work in blue-chip companies. They want high salaries and stock options.

The ability to tolerate risk or, to put it another way, the ability to understand cyclicality and then adapt to change does not feature strongly on the MBA curriculum.

According to Henry Mintzberg:

> *Classrooms do not create entrepreneurial leaders, they create hubris.*

This view is supported by Warren Buffett, quoted earlier.

Highly-qualified, high-powered MBAs don't want to start small, or think small, and they are not taught to cope with repeated cyclical failure. Largely because they don't study the internal and external cycles of business adequately, they want to hit the ball out of the park every time; and that's not the way the real-time cyclical world of business works.

---

[11]   *Global Entrepreneurship Monitor 2003*, www.gemconsortium.org.

There are, of course, many successful, change-managing exceptions among business school alumni – but there is more than a grain of truth in Mintzberg's and Buffett's observations.

On a positive note, unlike people, in the cycle of human life, SME companies can experience a re-birth, and can emerge from the downward slide of decline, through re-invention and entrepreneurial flair. The likelihood, however, of such a beneficial outcome is increased greatly by deep understanding of the internal and external cycles that fundamentally affect all businesses. These natural cycles of change are remorseless, inevitable, massively influential – and massively ignored.

Some of the cycles and their effects that need to be considered by the SME leadership team are:

- Operating cycle.
- Strategic cycle.
- Stakeholder cycle.
- Leadership cycle.
- Innovation cycle.
- Sales cycle.
- Product cycle.
- Managerial cycle.
- People cycle.
- Assets cycle.

The benefits from an appreciation of the dynamics of these cycles lie in the understanding of how their alignment can affect business results directly. This understanding, followed by a process of pro-active implementation of change, is a large portion of the work of SME leaders.

We illustrate the concept by considering the essential features in any basic business transactional cycle:

- Vision.
- Team-building.
- Selling.

- Managing.
- Innovation.

Examination of these features, and their relationships, forms the conceptual basis for our STAR leadership model.

3
THE STAR LEADERSHIP MODEL

To operate effectively and profitably, transactional cycles of any significant scale require the structure of an organisation, the application of management and appropriate leadership. In the real world of business, whether red-in-tooth-and-claw SME entrepreneurship or high-minded, altruistic not-for-profit organisations, leadership also follows a similar pattern, mirroring the cyclical model of transactions:

- **Vision** takes the original idea, articulates its future and inspires those who will be part of the implementation team.
- **Building the team** into an effective, efficient, multi-functional delivery group is the next task of the leader.
- The following leadership stage in the cycle is **selling**, where the organisation must find the right customers to ensure its growth.
- Then **management** becomes the dominant feature of the leadership cycle, as the growing business requires the input of systems, processes and measurement to deliver all-important profitability.
- Some of this profit will then go to fund the development of further novel approaches and, thus, continue the cycle of inputs through **innovation**.

We have worked with hundreds of SME leaders and entrepreneurs in Ireland, the UK and world-wide. They came in all shapes, sizes and varieties, from inventors with a bright idea, hard-working people with a dream, hustlers who could sell anything, executives in multi-national companies wanting to break out on their own, and teams using their complementary skills to implement exciting projects.

We have run formal entrepreneurship programmes for government economic development agencies; spoken at leadership conferences and seminars; worked with the down-sizing programmes of multi-national corporations, in preparing executives for enforced entrepreneurial futures; consulted on business start-up and development with individual SME leaders; and run specific programmes for female entrepreneurial leaders.

We have also coached many top teams, and their individual executives, in the attitudes and skills required for the leadership of growing SMEs.

Working with such diversity is interesting, complex, sometimes frustrating, and frequently challenging, but it provides a rich accessible mine of information on SME leaders:

- Who are they?

- What makes them succeed – or fail?

- How can meaning and direction be derived from the seeming chaos of their varied and challenging daily lives?

- How can the massive amount of information about often complex individuals, and their sometimes frenetic work lives, be distilled into an understandable, communicable form?

- How do leadership teams of stellar-growth SMEs learn?

Years of work, observation, analysis and experience gives us an understanding that has helped many to find answers to the problems they encounter on the SME leadership journey.

Our own, sometimes painful, experience brings caution as to how those answers are applied but, nevertheless, clear trends and categories are apparent.

THE STAR LEADERSHIP MODEL

We have articulated these learnings in the simple, yet powerful, STAR leadership model. It has been applied, with repeated successful effect, in many business situations.

To improve the performance of leaders and their entrepreneurial leadership teams, we first need to understand the thinking, motivation, needs, beliefs, actions and characteristics of the diverse individuals who make up these value-creating groups.

Entrepreneurial leaders come from highly varied, sometimes surprising backgrounds, and academics, writers and commentators have come up with a wide, and often complex, range of classifications in order to facilitate analysis.

Our STAR model places entrepreneurial leaders clearly and logically in five main categories, correlated to the business transactional model:

- Visionaries.
- Team-builders.
- Sellers.
- Managers.
- Innovators.

We also observe a sixth group of rare individuals – Wild-Cards. While they cannot be classified readily, or their characteristics included easily in any operating model, they cannot be ignored.

The STAR model is helpful in our work with individual leaders, as they assess strengths and weaknesses relative to their own entrepreneurial competence. It also assists them in playing to the specific strengths that give them their competitive edge. But its most powerful value lies in guiding the building of a robust leadership top team, with the full complement of essential leadership attributes required for the achievement of stellar growth.

Uniquely, the STAR model builds leadership for the specific market situation in which the SME competes.

Each attribute type in the model represents a leadership force or vector, clearly observable to varying degrees in entrepreneurial leadership activities. These forces are evident in enterprises, personalities and teams.

While most people have predominant characteristics, placing them clearly in one or two of the five main categories, they will also exhibit significant but lesser traits in the other categories.

Visionary leader

This category of leader has a relatively high chance of developing a successful stellar-growth SME. The Visionary leader is the public's perception of the classic entrepreneur – ambitious, with grand visions; highly energetic; seemingly workaholic in risk-laden pursuit of big objectives, committed, with a driving belief in self; and convinced that they can control their destiny and shape the future of others.

In the words of W.E. Henley:

It matters not how strait the gate,
How charged with punishments the scroll,
I am the master of my fate,
I am the captain of my soul.

Visionaries are inspirational leaders and overtly confident – leading with the big vision.

Team-builder leader

If the Visionary leader brashly leads from the front, the Team-builder leader leads with the top team, as a first among equals. Team-builders have magnetic charisma and empathetic judgement, which enable the creation of high-achieving teams. But they are impatient with poor performance, and will root out and discard ruthlessly members of the team who consistently under-perform.

Team-builders are highly respected by their team colleagues – leading with collegial pride.

Seller leader

Like the Team-builders, Sellers are tremendous networkers, with a great empathy for people. They want to create solutions for their customers, develop their employees and generally assist all with whom they come in contact. They are highly-effective social animals. People want to do business with them. They are convinced of the key importance of selling and will train, motivate, support and invest heavily in their sales force.

They are sales leaders and create great loyalty – leading with the big sale.

Manager leader

This category of leader has a high chance of business success. They are driven by efficiency, are ruthlessly cost-conscious and financially-literate. Power and control gives them an adrenalin rush. They are often highly-effective marketers, good at process, good at sales. Of all the leader categories in our model, they have the highest success rate at leading an SME from its early stages into, and through, a period of stellar growth.

They are growth leaders with a strong focus on the numbers – leading with orderly security.

Innovator leader

Inventions, ideas, gizmos, gadgets, novelties – many inventors aspire to be successful in business, but relatively few actually make it to the point where they are leading their own SME. True innovator leaders have something else: an awareness that an invention, or a novel business model, is nothing without implementation – and implementation requires wider skills than those of the innovator alone. They are great lateral thinkers: highly enthusiastic about their novel ideas, as well as technically literate and technologically competent.

They are technical leaders and intensely intelligent – leading with the big idea.

Each of the five types in the STAR model has a distinct leadership persona, though it is true that most individuals show strong attributes of more than one type. Key lessons can be drawn on how each category handles its function successfully, but more important is how these facets of the SME leadership personality are brought together intellectually, organisationally and operationally to create competitive advantage and growth.

We refer to these five types as dynamic vectors of stellar-growth. They bring value-adding competitive advantage to the individual entrepreneurial leader and the members of the SME top team.

Wild-Card leaders

Sometimes, we are faced with individuals who do not easily fit the patterns of Visionary, Team-builder, Seller, Manager or Innovator. It is difficult to advise and help these misfits because, in addition to the facts that their strengths are hard to identify clearly and their weaknesses seem overwhelming, they simply don't give a damn.

However, experience and intuition overrides our scepticism with regard to the Wild-Cards. We don't know how to advise them, but we work with them as best we can – we just know they'll make it somehow.

Often, they are better understood with the benefit of hindsight and, when they have led the company to success, the tales they tell at conferences can be highly entertaining.

They are different leaders – leading with sheer bloody-mindedness.

STAR LEADERSHIP CATEGORIES & TEAM-WORK

Perfection in any facet of business life belongs to the world of theory and, theoretically, the fully-implemented Star leadership model is the ultimate perfect top team. It encompasses all the positive characteristics of the disciplined, intuitive, flexible, responsive selling entrepreneur. Its implementation demonstrates total commitment towards achievement of goals, and has the ability to forge powerful enduring personal relationships.

The model helps the creation of a mutually-beneficial shared vision of the nuclear goals, and guides the team so that it delivers efficiently, and continually rewards its customers with positive innovation.

Such a complementary team is perfectly aligned to the needs of the informal, but demanding, selling environment, created and driven by the individual business-to-business buyer or end-user.

In terms of entrepreneurship, organisation design, team-working and customer contact, the Star leadership model enables a clear focus on key issues, far beyond that normally employed by the traditional process-driven management team.

The design, construction and operation of the model evolved from our involvement over years of observation, research, consulting and our own practice of leadership, management, selling and entrepreneurship. We have also drawn from the published works of leading authors on team-building and people-management.

Arguably, the most influential and helpful guidance available to us for a robust understanding of theoretical team-building is based on the powerful research of Dr Meredith Belbin. His ground-breaking work on team-building, team performance, and team roles has been used successfully by thousands of companies in creating successful management teams, and its accurate insights have been invaluable in the creation of the STAR leadership top team model.

In the Belbin model,[12] most people have a natural primary role, one they usually play in whatever teams they join. Many also have secondary roles they can play if these roles are not filled by other team members, or if their own primary role is more effectively filled by another member. In a small team they will play a combination of roles.

The role that each person finds it most natural to adopt will depend on a number of psychological traits: the degree to which they are introvert or extrovert, the degree to which they are calm or highly strung, the degree to which they are dominant or submissive, and their level of intelligence. Other aspects of the individual will also have an influence; their maturity, their instinct to trust or suspect others, their tolerance of uncertainty, and so on.

Belbin developed the theoretical ability to design 'perfect' teams and coined the phrase:

"Nobody's perfect, but a team can be".

We would stop well short of claiming that the STAR leadership model can help create perfection. However, the analytic clarity it brings to top team formation gives SMEs access to a means of dramatically accelerating their chances of putting together a leadership team capable of achieving ambitious stellar goals.

---

12   R. Meredith Belbin, *Management Teams: Why They Succeed or Fail*, Butterworth-Heinemann, 2003.

The specific operational demands and objectives of our leadership STAR model means that it must be designed and operated in a highly specified way. It does not attempt to put together the pieces for a 'perfect' team with specified roles in the Belbin sense, because its closeness to reality carries characteristics of the fundamental ambiguity and paradox of business.

It seems to go against all natural order, in that while the model creates a group, functioning with positive group-think, yet it can be applied operationally with the complex, radical, sometimes anarchistic single-mindedness of the entrepreneur / leader.

STAR functions as a high-performance team structure within which the goals of the SME are central and powerful drivers. Synergistic added value is delivered by coordinated performance of the five key leadership growth vectors in the STAR model.

BALANCING THE VECTORS WITHIN THE TEAM

Despite the fact that business is a complex activity, whether pursued in an SME or global corporation context, our STAR model's fundamental categories, or vectors, of leadership are conceptually clear, and simple to apply in any business. They are visionary, team-building, selling, managing and innovating leadership.

The presence of all these forces are essential over time if stellar growth is to be achieved, but SMEs are often unaware of this. In failing to augment or balance under-performing teams, companies regularly fail to grow as strongly as their potential would allow.

SME leaders themselves, are in our experience likely to be well-intentioned and are strongly motivated towards being part of a forceful top team driving their company on a stellar-growth trajectory, but the large number of behavioural traits essential to success, are at best only partly identified and partly understood.

In addition to having a somewhat blinkered view of how to frame the true situation on leadership implementation in the SME, their problem in seeking improvement often lies in finding a robust, yet simple, guidance mechanism.

Amidst all the urgent complexity of running a stellar-growth SME, the leader needs a model with characteristics which enable him to balance the top team, and in particular, to identify the weak areas in his own leadership capability.

The STAR leadership model provides a tool to:

- Help in evaluating the current overall leadership strength in the company – including the personal strengths of the entire top team.
- Provide benchmark standards applicable to the competitive situation in which the company operates.
- Identifies the vital gaps where improvement must be made.
- Defines the areas of training, development or recruitment necessary to the establishment of a balanced, competitive team.

The STAR leadership model shows the way clearly and identifies problems in a comprehensive yet user-friendly way. The individual requirements of each leadership vector are measured by assessing 20 key leadership behaviours in each category.

This proven mechanism for individual assessment, team evaluation, team building and stellar-growth goal achievement is the STAR leadership model.

In considering the five dimensions – and, for completeness, also looking at the dimension we cannot fit into our model, the Wild-Card – we:

- Describe their general characteristics.
- Examine the dark side of each dimension.
- Look at the effect of the key behaviours.
- Describe the application of our leadership measurement process.
- Look at the balance of a STAR leadership team.

At the end of each chapter dedicated to a vector, we have included a scoring table, where, having considered the hands-on experiences of our exemplar leaders, you can identify the extent that you personally identify with each facet or characteristic. Rigorously mark yourself on a scale of 1 to 5 – be ruthlessly honest – and fill in the numbers on the tables.

Later we will show you how to carry out the same exercise for all the members of your top team, and how to assess the leadership situational needs for your company.

You can do all this from the guidance in this book but, for our comprehensive expert analysis, at a reasonable cost, go on-line to **www.linkubator.com/star** and follow the input instructions.

We will analyse your data and give you a thorough diagnosis of your own leadership behaviours, relative to the competitive situation in which your company operates.

4
THE VISIONARY LEADER

In the 1960s, and with later work in the 1980s, David McClelland of Harvard University suggested that individuals driven by high personal-achievement levels had a particularly strong potential for success in entrepreneurship and business leadership. Visionary leaders are high achievers, and the visionary is the public's perception of the classic entrepreneur: ambitious, with grand visions, highly energetic and seemingly workaholic, in risk-laden pursuit of big objectives.

The visionary is highly committed to the company but, most importantly, has a driving belief in self and his or her own ability to deliver results. He or she is very self-confident, self-reliant and sure that his or her own way is the best way to shape his or her own future and the future of others.

Ivan McCabry the majority shareholder in Mivan, a highly successful international construction business, began trading in 1975 on his own, recruiting Mervyn McCall a year later.

Ivan is the 'face' of Mivan to his staff and the outside world. More significantly, he is an inspiring visionary leader, who personally has trained and developed his highly-skilled staff in line with his vision to help him to build Mivan into the international success it is today.

Visionaries also have a defining conviction that they are masters of their own destiny and in control of their lives. More particularly, a distinguishing characteristic is that they will resist being controlled by other people, or other things beyond their influence. They take pride in the fact that they personally can make a difference, and they cherish the freedom and flexibility to go their own way.

While they are high profile individuals, and ideally prefer to run their own lives free from the supervision of others, they sometimes find their early success and, indeed, obtain their business training in working for large corporations, where submission to the control of others is mandatory. However, their release and salvation often comes whenever they look for freedom in leading their own new entrepreneurial ventures.

They are inspirational leaders and have a sometimes positive, sometimes negative, need to take most of the individual credit for themselves. This can fly in the face of the need for co-operation and teamwork within a STAR leadership team.

Because of this fixation with themselves, visionaries see the efforts that they expend on their company in a strongly personal light. The company is them; they are the company. While this attitude can be hard to live with for other people working in the company top team, the visionary's driving self-belief and commitment often leads to the setting of challenging stretch goals.

It also delivers the vital motivational role modelling that inspires the entire SME to unanticipated levels of exemplary high-performance achievement.

Visionaries set big hairy audacious goals; they shoot for the moon; they reach for the stars; they have great ambitions – any metaphor you care to use. The feature that distinguishes successful visionary entrepreneurial leaders from idle dreamers is that they plan obsessively. Their plans may seem wild and extreme but, typically, they contain clear ambitious goals and will be executed ruthlessly, sometimes at great pain to people who get in the way, or are perceived as being in the way.

Visionary entrepreneurs are often very impatient with government agencies, bankers, unions, venture capitalists and any organisation or body that does not conform to the sovereign will of the visionary entrepreneurial leader.

Visionaries may be hard to live with but, arguably, they are the key drivers behind the economic success of the entire capitalist system.

VISIONARY LEADERS – THE DARK SIDE

Most of the visionary leaders we have known are honourable, capable people, who serve their communities well and contribute positively to mankind in general. But there are exceptions, and even those who do much good can sometimes go off-track.

The strong need for achievement in visionary leaders is related to the requirement for regular feedback or acknowledgement of their impact on the business. In order to maximise the number of such responses, they are constantly putting out fires, dealing with crises and wearing many hats within the business. They like to be seen as number one, to be recognised and given prominence for their achievements.

Manfred Kets de Vries, of Insead Business School in Paris, has observed that many top leaders are narcissists.[13] While having a high level of self-esteem and self-worth is helpful to all of us in our lives, and not only to visionary entrepreneurs, those with an exaggerated sense of their own superiority and talent may suffer costly consequences, as did Narcissus himself. But it should come as no surprise that narcissists may become powerful leaders in political and corporate affairs.

Winston Churchill was one such, and demonstrated the power of a visionary leader in leading Britain defiantly, particularly in the early dark days of World War II. Many narcissists are highly talented people, with risk-taking capabilities that would frighten the life out of less enterprising individuals. But, while self-belief is a wonderful thing, self-absorption is not so helpful or attractive, and can be indicative of a lack of empathy for other people.

The visionary entrepreneurs to whom we have been exposed over the years can often be highly sensitive to criticism, in that it threatens the self-image that they have so carefully constructed.

Like Churchill, they are right all the time – even when they are wrong. The catastrophic, wasteful, and ill-considered strategy of the Dardanelles Campaign in World War I demonstrates the dark

---

[13] In Greek mythology, Narcissus was a beautiful young man, who, on looking in the water, fell in love with his own reflection.

narcissistic side of Winston Churchill. As First Sea Lord of the Admiralty, he was responsible for and, indeed, championed this strategic blunder in the face of strong opposition. The same doggedness and determination that produced the positive will to resist in World War II cost tens of thousands of lives in the Dardanelles in World War I.

Robert Maxwell, the notorious publishing tycoon, Ernest Saunders, the disgraced former head of Guinness, more recently the corrupt Bernie Ebbers of WorldCom and the manipulative peer Conrad Black, all have demonstrated that immense visionary talent is no antidote to the destructive influence of self-deluding narcissism.

The dark side of the visionary entrepreneur is well exemplified in the case of Kenneth Lay of Enron, as described by Matt Haig in the book, *Brand Failures*[14] and, while this massive corporation was certainly no SME, the lessons of its fall from grace provide learning for visionary leaders in any size of enterprise.

L ittle remains to be said that has not already been well-publicised about the rise, and scandalous, fall of Texan energy giant, Enron. In the relatively short space of 15 years, under the aggressive visionary leadership of Ken Lay, Enron rose from being an inconsequential SME to become the seventh largest company in the United States, and the best-known energy supplier in the world. It boasted over 21,000 employees and had a presence in more than 40 countries.

As well as generating energy, the firm also generated a powerful brand identity. It won *Fortune* magazine's award for 'Most Innovative Company in America' six years running, and was also high in the rankings for the same magazine's 'Best Companies to Work For' chart. The company projected an image of being a good corporate citizen and published a social and environmental report that looked at the moves it was taking with regard to the environmental consequences of its business, its employee relations and, most ironically, its anti-corruption and bribery policies.

---

[14] Matt Haig, *Brand Failures: The Truth Behind the 100 Biggest Branding Mistakes of All Time*, Kogan Page, 2003.

Over the years, Enron depicted itself as a professionally-led, highly-profitable, growing company. Of course, in 2001, this turned out to be a lie – one of the biggest in global corporate history. The company's profit statements were proved to be untrue, and it emerged that massive debts had been hidden so that they weren't evident in the company's accounts.

Enron's accountancy firm, Arthur Andersen, was involved in the shredding of documents relating to Enron's accounts, which was catastrophic for that firm's reputation as well. As the depth of the deception unfolded, investors and creditors retreated, forcing the firm into Chapter 11 bankruptcy in December 2001. When the facts came to light, Enron executives made matters worse by refusing to testify and arguing that they had no chance of a fair trial.

The Enron scandal also had political implications, because of the firm's close links with the White House. Enron ploughed millions of dollars into George Bush's 2000 election campaign. Although Bush was a personal friend of Enron's CEO, Kenneth Lay, he was quick to distance himself from any direct involvement with the firm.

The long-term effects of the scandal will be felt for years to come, though the Enron name is already beyond repair and forever likely to be synonymous with 'corporate irresponsibility'.

Kenneth Lay was certainly a visionary entrepreneur. The hubris that led to his downfall is a singular warning to all entrepreneurs and business leaders not to believe too much of their own publicity. It is note-worthy, and somewhat chilling with hindsight, to consider the Enron strap-line, 'Thinking the unthinkable and attaining the impossible'. These were the thoughts that formed the basis of goal-setting for Lay and his top team.

Not only did Kenneth Lay fall but the collapse, first of Enron, and then of its accounting firm Arthur Andersen, created a shock within the worldwide business community of analogous proportions to the horror of the Twin Towers collapse of 9/11. Two of the most powerful brand edifices in the world, the giant Enron, and the upstanding Arthur Andersen, gone completely, disappeared.

Matt Haig's opinion is that, if it was about anything, the Enron scandal was about accountancy. Specifically, it was about shredding documents relating to Enron's accounts and concealing massive debts, a fact that immediately implied a considerable element of complicity on the part of the accountancy firm. This complicity was implied further when David Duncan, Enron's chief auditor at Andersen, appeared involuntarily at the first investigation into the scandal and then refused to speak in order to avoid incriminating himself. Even when Joseph Berardino, Andersen's chief executive, vigorously defended his firm's role in the affair, he was unable to undo the damage. Once it was found guilty of deliberately destroying evidence, the firm suffered severe brand damage and the tremors were felt throughout the entire accountancy profession.

This story of the dark side of visionary leadership is highlighted because of its extremes of behaviour and the lessons they can bring to the SME and its top team leadership. When visionary leadership becomes destructive megalomania.

Now after those warnings, on the positive side, the virtues of most SME visionary leaders far outweigh any negative points. The key entrepreneurial leadership benefits and activities that they bring to their company and its top team are vital to the company's growth.

The four over-arching Visionary leadership behaviours measured in the Star model are:

- Visioning.
- Strategising
- Energising
- Deciding.

VISIONING

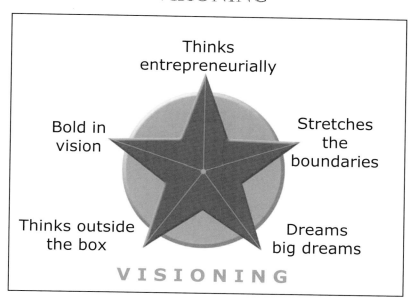

1. Thinks entrepreneurially

An entrepreneurial outlook is a vital asset for the Visionary leader of an SME. All growth companies need lightning responses to opportunity in order to maintain competitive advantage; allied to a native cunning in applying the commitment of appropriate resources, this will allow a strong profit.

The hallmark of the entrepreneur is the ability to trade, to buy and, in particular, to sell, while retaining a good margin. The way to achieve this objective is often by being well ahead of the pack and seeing where the market is going, before the masses pile in and destroy the value-adding opportunity.

The best entrepreneurial thinkers re-act almost intuitively to stimulus and, therefore, there is little scope for educating someone to be a top performer in this behaviour area. Nonetheless, any leader can sharpen their performance by keeping themselves alert to changes and considering pro-actively opportunities for stealing a march on competitors.

One of the highest-profile entrepreneurial thinkers and role models is Richard Branson, who has started and built dozens of SMEs. His rapid thought-processes have enabled him to grow a business empire across a range of totally unrelated areas, from airlines to wedding retailers, to financial services, and many more. The good news is that, while very few SME Visionary leaders will attain the heights of entrepreneurial success achieved by an outstanding thinker like Branson, entrepreneurial thinking can be developed by conscious will, to a greater or lesser degree.

Individuals can be inspired to think entrepreneurially by role models who have done it successfully. Richard Branson is certainly a high-achieving role model and, yet, in the many entrepreneurship programmes we have run for small businesses, we have been privileged to hear SME leaders tell stories that, for passion and inspirational value, rate alongside the best tales of the creator of the Virgin empire.

2. Stretches the boundaries

One of the great challenges of leaders in the context of an SME is to get people to recognise the reality of their situation in terms of available resources and yet, at the same time, to strive to achieve stretch goals that, at first sight, appear to be beyond them. The ability to create wealth beyond known resources is the fundamental mark of the entrepreneurial leader.

There is a fine balance between setting stretch goals, which to those who must deliver them are clearly not achievable, and setting stretch goals, which as challenging targets will inspire a greater effort to ensure their attainment.

The importance of role-modelling, personified by the individual setting corporate targets, cannot be overstated. Example is one of the strongest motivators available to the business leader as he tries to take his team in pursuit of rich goals.

T ake the case of a managing director like Peter Doherty of GDS, the Irish market leader in garage doors, who sets aggressive sales goals for his sales team. But, if a salesman is struggling to meet targets, Peter will get in his car and drive hundreds of miles to visit customers with him in a committed effort to see the challenging goals achieved.

Even if that particular intervention fails, in time as a team they succeed, due to the fact that Peter's inspirational support in trying alongside his salespeople validates the meaning of targets – gaining commitment from everyone in chasing the stretch goals for the following month.

Stretching the boundaries, however, is about much more than setting high sales targets. Nokia, where a mundane business was re-invented completely, is a graphic illustration of the power of visionary leadership in stretching the boundaries of thinking.

3. Dreams big dreams

A dream is a vision and a big vision is a big dream. Big dreams are essential for the SME leader who wants to achieve the stellar growth which, just maybe, will form the foundation for an enterprise that one day can take on the world and become a global giant.

T o Sir Michael Smurfit belongs the honour of being the first Irish entrepreneur to achieve world-recognised status. With the onward march of the Celtic Tiger, he has been followed by many whose big dreams have become a demonstrable reality, as they confidently lead industries and sectors across the business spectrum.

But Michael dreamed the big dream in an Ireland where such dreaming was dismissed as lunacy, and it is the measure of his achievement that he took a little SME boxmaker to the point where it could compete with the greatest corporations in the global paper industry. Michael Smurfit transmitted his big dream to his top team, and thousands of Irish people, who then made his dream their dream; with his visionary leadership, they took the Jefferson Smurfit Group into a premier position on the world business stage.

Because he was the first, Sir Michael's achievement must be recognised for its watershed significance, not only for the company itself and its people, but also for its impact on the emerging Irish economy and the nascent dreams, small and big, of thousands of newly-hopeful Irish entrepreneurs.

4. Thinks 'outside the box'

Dreaming big dreams is one thing, thinking 'outside the box' is another distinct aspect of visioning. It refers not to the size or scale of the ambition, but to radical lateral thought, which sees patterns and connective elements that are invisible to most observers. The ability to see where others cannot, and to recognise special opportunity where others see only boring incrementalism, brings many rewarding chances to a growing SME.

It is not enough for the Visionary leader to think laterally from time to time. A characteristic of the real 'out of the box' thinker is that he or she is never off-duty, even when in social situations. They are recognisable by their ability to see the bizarrely humorous in the most humdrum settings and can be extremely entertaining company, even when their fast-track minds are latching on to a valuable new thought.

Sean Quinn is Ireland's richest man, having created a €3 billion empire by building a series of diverse activities into a powerful synergistic conglomerate, covering aggregates, cement, glass, packaging, radiators, financial services, hotels and international property.[15]

Founded in 1973, the origins of the Quinn Group lie in the supply of sand and gravel to local builders and farmers. Throughout the 1970s, the company developed its product range, with the quarrying of aggregates, the production of ready-mix cement, the manufacture of concrete blocks and the establishment of a concrete products manufacturing plant in Williamstown, Co Galway.

From this successful base, the group expanded into the national market in the 1980s with the establishment of a rooftile factory, a

---

[15] www.quinn-group.ie.

pre-stressed concrete factory and a 0.5 million tonnes *per annum* cement works at Derrylin, complemented in 2000 by the opening of the group's second cement works at Ballyconnell, Co Cavan.

The 1990s saw further expansion, with additional manufacturing operations in polystyrene products, bituminous tar, aircrete blocks and two of the most modern container glass plants in the world. Hand-in-hand with the development of its manufacturing operations, the group expanded its international property portfolio.

The Quinn Group's general insurance company has become a major player in the insurance industry in Ireland and has expanded into pensions, investments and healthcare.

In a recent conversation with Sean, Will formed the view that his 'outside the box' leadership thinking is the secret of the stellar growth of Sean's companies. The down-to-earth style of this tremendously successful, yet engagingly modest, man belies the speed and prowess of his lateral thinking.

5. Bold in vision

The Visionary leader is not only an entrepreneurial thinker, stretching the boundaries, dreaming big dreams and seeing things others can't see, he is also bold, forthright and direct. This visionary boldness characteristic is applied sparingly, but with great impact. In addition to the competitive advantage delivered to the SME by the force of value-adding execution, the motivational effect on its staff is electric.

When used after careful thought, and implemented with a coolness of approach, boldness of vision can result in the transformation of a company's future.

In the late 1980s, the Irish linen industry was in serious decline, with thousands of jobs disappearing every year and once-great companies, some of them well over 100 years old, going out of business. Many of these failing entities had been trading all over the world and, in addition to the fact that they were household names in the textile industry, the long-established families who owned them were the commercial aristocracy of Northern Ireland.

One such company was Thomas Ferguson Ltd of Banbridge, a linen weaver with a world-wide reputation for manufacturing fine double-damask Irish linen. The business had reached the end of the road and looked like joining many of its peers in oblivion. Its markets were shrinking, technology and systems were decades out of date, staff and employees were deflated and the cost-base was unsustainably high. The future was inevitable closedown, with the loss of skilled employment to the area, and the demise of a once-proud 150-year-old company.

Ralph Bauer was managing director of Franklins, a small woven-badge manufacturer, also in Banbridge. He alone had the boldness of vision to see a future for Thomas Ferguson. Against strong advice, he acquired the business and courageously implemented a visionary growth strategy. He invested in state-of-the-art weaving technology, aggressive branding and change management, resulting in survival and subsequent success. His words convey the commitment and passion that underpinned his bold decision-making:

> *"Being a manufacturer gives me great satisfaction – to see products in dispatch, about to be shipped to a customer, knowing that they are a combination of materials, expertise, effort, time and organization – and will result in payment.*
>
> *Many have similar enjoyment, but why did we succeed and others not? The answer lies in a combination of luck, circumstance, innovation, diligence, detail, learning from experience, risk-taking, bloody-mindedness and ignorance.*
>
> *To be competitive, we had to change Fergusons, we had to develop software to enable a reduction in design time from four to six months to 45 minutes, to reduce loom change time from four hours to 35 seconds.*
>
> *We bought new looms that, contrary to received wisdom, allowed us the flexibility to manufacture 'tailor-made' or 'bespoke' products (mass customization, although we did not know that consultant-speak phrase then). We reduced our looms from over 100 to less than 10 without loss of production and reduced the manufacturing area by 90%.*
>
> *We had commissioned a consultant to undertake a market investigation before purchasing Fergusons. Once the purchase was complete, we adopted the report's advice, discontinued over half of the products (those we considered to be commodity products and subject to severe price competition) and we went 'up market'. As*

planned, reduced sales turnover resulted – imagine the horror with which banks and others viewed our projections showing lower sales (with sardonic exasperation, we offered to project increasing fictional sales and increasing realistic losses).

*However, we stuck to **our** projections – profits, and more importantly, our cash flows, improved.*

In general, had we known beforehand – though due diligence had been properly undertaken – what we were going to let ourselves in for, we would never have bought Fergusons, for the worms continued to creep from the woodwork for years afterwards.

Fortunately, we didn't know. The most exhilarating experiences of my career took place and, more importantly, had we not gone ahead with the Ferguson purchase and innovation, Franklins would not exist today."

Today, with the Irish textile industry almost obliterated, Thomas Ferguson is the only remaining Irish linen double-damask weaver in the world and its superb linens grace the tables of royalty and the international super-rich. All thanks to Ralph Bauer's boldness of vision, speed of action and sure-footed execution.

STRATEGISING

Sets ambitious goals

Builds new concepts

Spots opportunities

Researches meticulously

Plans methodically

STRATEGISING

1. Sets ambitious goals

It is one thing to stretch the boundaries of vision through inspirational leadership, whether vocal or by role-model example, and quite another to set ambitious goals within a written operational plan. Such goals will have their origin in robust research with deep, detailed appreciation of the industry, its competitive landscape and the internal operations of the SME itself.

Selecting the range of goals is a difficult enough task in itself, but ranking them in order of importance and prioritising them with regard to their urgency brings a demanding discipline to the strategising leader's judgemental options. Getting this ambitious goal-setting wrong can skew not only the written plan, but can lead to under-performance in operations if goals are set too low, or can kill motivation if they are set too high.

For these reasons, once the vision is set, the strategising leader will involve the top team fully, in the evolution of thoroughly-researched and thoroughly-debated operating goals, which over time deliver on the vision. A key contributor to the successful achievement of such rich goals lies in the full involvement of the top team in their formation, and hence their crucial buy-in to the intellectual integrity of the targets themselves.

While all this sounds obvious, in the real world, it is not as easily delivered as it sounds, and the process demands a high level of strategising leadership to ensure success.

R ichard Chapman, CEO of £8 million software company, Skyline Systems, had a fight on his hands between two trusted executives on his four-person top team. We were called in to help him to resolve a dispute that was escalating out of control, to the extent that it was seriously threatening Richard's leadership.

The protagonists were from Finance and Sales respectively, with a number of the more junior members of staff backing each side. This was not the first time that we had seen Finance and Sales departments square up to one another, though mostly it is just a healthy tension; in this case, it was becoming a pathological problem.

Simply put, the row was over agreed sales goals the team had created. The sales people were prepared to go for these targets, but they required higher financial resource commitments in order to sign off on them. Needless to say, the finance people wanted to cut the resource committal goals, because they 'did not really believe the sales goals would be met'. And, at the time, the company was strapped for cash. Stalemate.

In this case, we advised Richard that he had to take the position of strategising leader. All the research that had gone into the goal-setting could not resolve the stand-off, and only he could move this less than clear-cut situation forward.

He stuck with the sales goals, keeping the pressure on the sales team, and increased the resource committal, at the same time giving the finance team the challenging ambitious goal of going out to find the increased funding. His strategy gave an equally-matched challenge to both opposing parties, thus turning their attention to delivering rich, focussed goals and away from futile butting of heads.

Richard had a lonely decision to make but he did not compromise on his strategic responsibility to set ambitious goals.

2. Spots opportunities

Successful strategising essentially is about making good choices on opportunities, and good judgement on their implementation. Therefore, it is logical that, assuming a consistency of quality on the choices and judgement, the more opportunities spotted, the better for the future of the SME.

The strategising leader spots more opportunities than her competitors, though it takes effort to find them. Reading trade magazines and targeted browsing of the Internet; trudging exhaustedly round enormous fairs and exhibitions; a seemingly endless round of networking dinners and business lunches; time-consuming training and development courses – all hard, hard work, but it pays off for the strategising leader.

Through hard work and great entrepreneurial talent, Rotha Johnston and her husband Henry built Variety Foods to become one of the most successful food-service companies in Ireland, and subsequently sold it in a highly-successful exit.

Prior to her involvement in Variety Foods, Rotha had worked at director level in Northern Ireland's economic development agency and was instrumental in helping scores of fast-growth SMEs with their innovation programmes. When she was leading her own business, her entrepreneurial skills and ability to spot opportunities for growth gave Variety Foods a competitive advantage in achieving stellar-growth.

In spotting opportunities, Rotha also used her expertise as a researcher to help her make the right choices and, from wide reading, information-gathering and deep market knowledge, she had the capability to apply good judgement to their exploitation.

For an SME, as indeed for any size of organisation, it is also vital to turn down opportunities that do not fit with the core strategy. It has been said that a business' strategy is defined more accurately by what it chooses not to do, rather than by what it does.

3. Plans methodically

From our experience of working with large companies such as Shell and Motorola, we came to an appreciation of their commitment to the importance of methodical planning. Shell was the pioneer of methodical scenario planning in the 1970s and 1980s and, for a period, at that time of turbulent volatility in the oil industry, it gave them a significant competitive advantage. Ultimately, their competitors caught up and today methodical modelling is an accepted day-to-day process for the vast majority of large corporations. Regrettably, the reverse is the case for most SMEs where planning, if carried out at all, is sporadic and anything but methodical.

Planning in SMEs has improved over the last 10 years, but it still has a long way to go. It simply does not work to leave the planning process to be carried out by the financial controller, who runs a few spreadsheets with budget numbers for the next year. However, not only is such abdication of leadership responsibility quite common, often even these basic numbers are not completed until several months of the period in question have elapsed.

There is no excuse for this situation, although we see it regularly in busy and reasonably successful firms, whose leaders are so occupied with driving production or sales that they do not take time to plan methodically. To remedy this defect would affect – positively and dramatically – their company's prospects for stellar-growth over time.

Folklore has it that SMEs are faster, more flexible and have other attributes that global corporations do not possess. While much of the folklore is true, in the area of methodical planning, smaller companies have a great deal to learn from giants like Shell.

Strategising leaders in many SME sectors have a real opportunity to achieve a similar relative competitive advantage to that enjoyed by Shell 30 years ago, simply because, if they plan methodically, they will be well ahead of most of their SME competition.

4. Researches meticulously

Good methodical plans need meticulous research and meticulous research takes time and money. In the real world of the SME, the strategising leader is faced with the problem of how to manage the ambiguity of matching detailed, time-consuming, thorough preparation with speed of action on implementation. He must avoid 'paralysis by analysis' at all costs.

General Colin Powell is quoted as saying that, if the information concerning a particular action falls in the range between 40% and 70%, then 'go with your gut instinct' and implement, rather than waste further time on diminishing returns of accuracy.

Creating a research project can be an opportunity for a leader to motivate the top team and to give them a challenging, time-bounded activity, with each person bringing information and analysis to the table, and participating in the joint assembly of the plan. This leadership approach is valuable, not only in the development of business plans, but in complex project work such as the preparation of complicated tenders, where meticulous research with effective division of labour and good teamwork is required.

K en Roulston, MD of Parity Ireland, an autonomous division of Parity PLC, frequently leads his top team in preparing multi-million pound tenders for public sector contracts. Ken is a strategising leader and researches meticulously, despite the tight time-frames within which these tenders have to be completed. He allocates responsibility to each member of the team and conducts regular joint review sessions to ensure that everything is coming together on time.

Inevitably, one section or other will be falling behind, but Ken redeploys his resources and puts pressure on the team to pull things back on track. As the deadline draws nearer, extra hours may have to be put in, the team may be working late, they may be in the office working all weekend, sustained by pizza and beer; the collegial enthusiasm within Ken's team is electric.

Throughout the intense, sometimes frenetic, process, Ken leads from the front by example – cajoling, encouraging, driving, challenging, counselling and contributing to the effort in the interest of speed of progress – but never, never compromising on the meticulous research process. In short, Ken manages the ambiguity.

When time is running out, he will make the hard decisions that are sometimes required in order to get the tender in on time, but his leadership on meticulous research gives Parity the best possible chance of a successful bidding outcome.

5. Builds new concepts

Building new concepts is a dimension of strategising leadership that comes readily to most SME founders. This is evidenced by the fact that they had the talent to develop the initial concept that led to the formation of their company in the first place. But there are obviously degrees of expertise.

I van McCabry of Mivan is an exemplar in this field. Mivan began trading as a sub-contractor on the Kilroot power station and Ivan built up the company on his visionary new concepts. The company diversified into general construction; specialised interiors for ships, shops and hotels; overseas contracting; formwork; house-building and property development. Flagship Mivan projects include the

Dome of the Rock mosque, Jerusalem; Euro Disney; P & O Cruises; the Scottish Parliament building; hotels in London and other testaments to Ivan's remarkable ability to build new concepts.

ENERGISING

Jack Welch measured his GE leaders by their ability to energise others. The STAR leadership model recognises the vital importance of this key dimension.

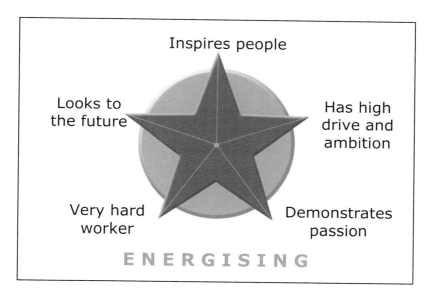

1. Inspires people

People can be inspired for a short time by a charismatic individual who has the ability to communicate in an attractive articulate manner, but will become quickly disillusioned if the message has little substance or if its proponent is shallow.

Inspiration requires the immediacy of charisma and articulate communication but, for it to be sustainable over time, it must also have a cause with which people can identify and engage passionately.

James Leckey owns and leads a successful SME. He has all the characteristics of a high profile leader and, as a former international rally driver, he has the image and panache of a fast-moving, exciting risk-taker. He is the type of individual who easily attracts attention and long-term followers, not only in the context of his sports interests, but also in his business.

But James is also something of an enigma. Somewhat surprisingly, this high-roller is driven by a passionate cause that usually would not be associated with his public persona. Leckey Design is a world-class leader in the design and manufacture of positioning equipment for children with cerebral palsy, muscular dystrophy, spina bifida and other special needs.

In 1982, James found his cause, when he was involved in a charity fund-raiser to provide positional aids for children. When the equipment arrived, James, who is a highly-skilled mechanical engineer, recognised that it fell well short of meeting the needs of the children and felt he could make great improvements.

Today, his successful and profitable company exports its products all over the world, a source of pride to both the workforce and management. The real energising inspiration, however, is found in the words of this committed, unusual leader:

> *"We believe creating their happiness is a serious business. Our degree of positional support gives children better opportunities to learn, play and have fun; their happiness is how we measure our success – the way it should be."*

Indeed.

2. Has high drive and ambition

Paul McWilliams is a farsighted business leader who recognised the early potential of IT. He led a talented team in building one of Ireland's most successful software and consulting companies, which he ultimately sold to a leading PLC.

Paul's own drive and ambition is self-evident, but the positive wealth-creating result of its application also has much to do with his ability to energise the top team in the companies of which he is chairman.

When asked for the secret of his success, Paul is quick to turn the attention away from himself:

> *"I have always believed that the best way to achieve ambitious goals in life is to surround yourself with driven, ambitious, successful people."*

His 'surrounding' strategy has an immediate energising effect on those who work for him, in that they feel part of Paul's own success and recognise that, by implication, their leader has identified them as successes in their own right.

There are further benefits from this association with drive and ambition. The energising leader also extends his ambitious reach, by involving and linking with leading personalities who demonstrate high drive and ambition in other businesses or influential positions. The networking value to his companies is enormous, and Paul's personal achievements bear witness to the effectiveness of his strategy.

3. Demonstrates passion

We have worked with numerous leaders of SMEs, and many CEOs and divisional vice-presidents of corporate behemoths. While, in many situations, their reactions are indistinguishable, as a generalisation our observation is that passionate commitment is significantly more in evidence in the SME leaders.

This may be due to their higher level of direct ownership or the relative longer service with the same company, but we suspect it may be more to do with the fact that the buck stops at a more personal level in most SMEs. The exceptions prove the rule – however, none better than Steve Ballmer of Microsoft.

S teve Ballmer's rousing presentations at the Microsoft conventions are unashamedly populist, brash, aggressive and clearly passionate performances. They create immediate energising responses from the vast TV audiences of Microsoft employees watching on giant screens worldwide.

Steve Jobs uses similar media, and equally passionate presentation, to energise the efforts of Apple and Disney employees.

The SME leader, with perhaps a much bigger relative stake in his own game, will demonstrate energising passion to those whom he is privileged to lead, despite the fact that he will address much smaller audiences.

Therein lies his greater relative power, because, however powerful a global TV presence appears on a giant screen, or however slick a Hollywood-produced choreography looks, it can never compete with a person-to-person chat, or direct eye-contact, or genuine passionate concern for individuals, delivered face-to-face.

4. Very hard worker

Gary Player's wry, deeply important but, by now, rather dog-eared comment that, the more he practised, the luckier he got, not only energises many golfers to work harder on improving the probability of Lady Luck smiling on them, but may well act as an incentive to SME leaders as they try to energise their teams. In the context of playing golf, practising is nothing short of plain hard work, so for individuals and companies the lesson is obvious.

An energising leader is likely to be perceived as the hardest grafter on the team, putting in long hours, and coping with superhuman loads of complex, demanding work. This individual will never be heard bleating plaintively about 'work/life balance'.

Stephen Kingon, currently chairman of InvestNI and formerly managing partner of PriceWaterhouseCoopers in Northern Ireland, is the epitome of such a leader. Recently, we travelled with him on a week-long business promotional visit to Denver, where our group arrived late in the afternoon and went out for a working dinner that evening.

At midnight, and tired after the flight, the rest of us went to bed, while Stephen went to work for three hours on his email. He arrived bright and breezy at 7am for an intense US-style breakfast meeting, after which he led the team in a series of back-to-back discussions throughout the day, which closed with another dinner, where he was the main speaker. Then he attended to several more hours of email.

So it went on for the entire week. When other members of the party, who, while busy, did not carry half Stephen's load, were visibly tiring, his high activity levels and positive attitude of leading from the front re-energised them and made the entire trip a great success.

Certainly, PriceWaterhouseCoopers is no SME but Stephen Kingon's hard-working approach underlines why, under his energising leadership, it grew to its position of outstanding competitive dominance in Northern Ireland.

5. Looks to the future

I had a friend was a big baseball player, back in High School,
He could throw that speedball by you, make you look like a fool, boy
Saw him the other night at this roadside bar, I was walkin' in he was walkin' out,
We went back inside, sat down, had a few drinks, but all he kept talking about, was Glory Days, well they'll pass you by,
Glory Days, in the wink of a young girl's eye,
Glory Days, Glory Days.

Bruce Springsteen's lyrics for his chart-topping hit *Glory Days* carry a poignancy with which we can all identify, whether way back then when we were the star player at the centre of attention, or part of the hero's admiring crowd.

While looking back to those golden times from the disappointed reality of today may bring a lump to the throat, the feelings engendered by The Boss's earthy lyrics are unlikely to energise, simply because they look to the past rather than the future.

STAR leadership in an SME must deliver energy, and energy comes from looking to the future, not to past triumphs, however glorious they may have been.

The Johnson's Coffee company has been roasting coffee in Belfast since 1913 and has survived and grown because its leadership, now in a fourth generation of the family, always have looked to the future throughout a turbulent century.

Over the years, their foresight has seen Johnson's develop innovative packaging with regular new product introductions, demonstrating an ability to adapt to changing customer tastes. Their leadership foresight has resulted in Johnson's premier position, when many less energetic competitors have fallen by the wayside in this crowded market.

This practice of far-sighted leadership behaviour, while exercised in a long-established industry, is paralleled by the example of innovative leadership demonstrated in the sunrise communications industries.

Leaders like the courageous Martha Lane Fox of LastMinute.com and hundreds of other entrepreneurs have looked to the future needs of consumers, developing and implementing the necessary solutions and, in the process, creating successful stellar-growth SMEs.

DECIDING

The deciding leader characteristic is the fourth dimension of the Visionary vector.

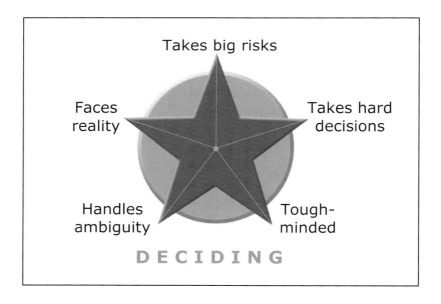

Every SME faces changes and its leaders have the imperative responsibility of making decisions on appropriate responses, which can condemn the enterprise to failure, or take it on a stellar-growth trajectory. To paraphrase Robert G. Ingersoll:

> *In business, as in nature, there are neither rewards nor punishments —*
> *there are only consequences.*

1. Takes big risks

Even the mightiest global corporations start as SMEs, and Richard Branson's multi-billion Virgin empire is no different. So we have no hesitation in using parts of Branson's story to illustrate the necessary risk-taking characteristics of the deciding SME leader.

Richard Branson started the Virgin mail-order record company when he was at Stowe public school, and took his first big risk when he opened an Oxford Street store at the age of 20. By the time he was 22, he had built a recording studio and recorded Mike Oldfield's five-million-selling album *Tubular Bells*.

In the next few years, Virgin Records signed The Rolling Stones, Culture Club, Janet Jackson, Peter Gabriel, Simple Minds, The Human League and many more top acts, which propelled Virgin well beyond the SME stage to become one of the world's top six record companies.

Branson was only 34, an immensely wealthy young man, with no need to risk anything. And then he risked it all, on the back of an out-of-the-blue phone call suggesting he set up an airline to carry passengers between London and New York.

Branson's fellow directors initially were surprised by the idea, and subsequently appalled when he announced that Virgin Atlantic would be up and running and fully operational within three months. This was a high-risk venture, which grew to become the second-largest long-haul carrier operating out of Heathrow and Gatwick, adding greatly to Virgin's profits and ultimately resulting in Branson's knighthood.

But even this pinnacle of recognition was not enough.

Sir Richard Branson has taken many huge risks, which have contributed to the stellar-growth of Virgin, but his derring-do does not end with business risk-taking. His ballooning escapades, one of which almost cost him his life off the coast of Ireland, and the record-breaking Blue Riband crossing of the Atlantic ocean, demonstrate the unique tolerance for risk of this decisive business leader.

2. Takes hard decisions

Many decisions with which a leader is faced are straightforward judgement choices, where logical deduction can make the selection of a particular course of action relatively simple. However, no deciding leader of a stellar-growth SME gets through a career without having to make some harsh, demanding, hard decisions.

In crisis, the hard decisions are numerous and the deciding leader needs strong resolve to withstand their crushing compound effect. But take the decisions he must, regardless of the pressure, as failure to decide is an abdication of the leadership with which he has been entrusted.

Weak leaders create a culture of indecisiveness, which allows the rapid spread of the virus of poor execution. Hence, arguably, it is better to risk making a bad decision rather than to vacillate or make no decision at all.

The hardest of the hard decisions are always those concerning people. There are a number of famous, and indeed notorious, leaders of corporate giants who are renowned or despised for their ability to take hard decisions: from Jack Welch who earned the nickname 'Neutron Jack' when he took the hard decisions in firing over 100,000 people to save and make a massive success of General Electric, to 'Chainsaw' Al Dunlap, whose slash-and-burn firing decisions enriched him personally, but mired Sunbeam in debt at the same time as throttling its operating ability.

The SME leader will not have to fire 100,000 people, but the decision to let five loyal long-serving machinists go can be just as hard. Or the case where a CEO we know had to close her fashion manufacturing unit in Dublin, while retaining the design, purchasing and sales people in employment. Seventy-eight long-term employees were paid off and their jobs 'exported' to Malaysia. This hard and emotionally-draining decision saved the company and the 27 remaining jobs.

3. Tough-minded

The deciding leader is tough-minded, in that leadership is not a short-term easy process, where a rousing speech from time-to-time is sufficient to see goals delivered. It is a grind, requiring constant reinforcement and the SME leader in the real world is aware, deep down, that when one set of problems have been resolved, others will arise in their place.

The need for 'tough-mindedness' is related directly to the fact that the leader first must lay the goals out in public and then have the mental and moral resilience to resist the inevitable clamour for compromise. This negative pressure can come from genuinely supportive colleagues with less vision or less appetite for work, or from the more sinister element, which is rampant within the public sector and also exists within a high proportion of businesses large and small, the non-aligned whose priority for 'work/life balance' takes precedence over the aims of the enterprise that pays their salary.

Toughness of mind enables the leader to get the team on-side, to push the decisions through in spite of minority internal opposition with which he will always be faced.

The tough-minded leader of an SME may also have to face down opposition from a surprising, but not uncommon, source – family shareholders. All CEOs live or die at the whim of the shareholders but, in most cases, their security is ensured by objective rationality, in that if they are delivering the results, everything is OK.

But 'family' firms can be different. Politicking and emotional dynamics may put a CEO under pressures that require the tough boss to apply the ultimate, but personally highly-threatening, sanction of offering his or her resignation. This issue needs consideration within SMEs, as the statistics show that only 25% survive beyond the second generation, and only 14% make it beyond the founder's grandchildren.

The Miller building company in Scotland is a case in point, where the current CEO Keith Miller, despite having led this Scottish company on a stellar-growth path, is under attack from his cousin James and a coalition of non-involved family shareholders who want to sell the company. Keith Miller is tough-minded; and he needs to be, to ensure the independent survival of this second-generation-managed company. He told the *Financial Mail*:

> *"I am personally very hurt, as you can imagine – the emotions here run very high. This is not a Mickey Mouse outfit. We turned the business around and we have done incredibly well. And we have done that because we are a private company and one with a strict level of professionalism and board corporate governance. I refuse to allow that to change. The rules we have in place for shares are designed to protect the company and to ensure it remains independent".*

Keith also said that, in the current year, the disgruntled family group had done very well in sharing generous dividends of £12 million:

> *"They are not on poor-street by any means. It is hugely disappointing this has ever got so far. I believe most of this could have been avoided completely".*

This tough-minded leader finished his interview with a resolute, self-assured, yet conciliatory, touch:

> *"Outside private equity buyers would be happy to buy but only with management support, which is out of the question. It will be very hard for someone to come in and buy that stake given that we won't be giving up control, and why should we? But this is a family company and we will find a way to get through this in the end".*

4. Handles ambiguity

If there is one attribute that demonstrates the value of experience in the 'University of Life' over the acknowledged value of a high-class, formal business education, it is the ability to make good decisions in the context of ambiguity.

Henry Mintzberg's assertion, quoted earlier, that university MBA classrooms produce hubris rather than leadership excellence goes somewhat further than we would want, but there is more than a grain of truth in what he says.

Sure, in a classroom, students can dissect all the theory of leadership and write theses on communication, motivation and negotiation, which gain top marks and, in due course, perhaps, a job in McKinsey, Bain or PwC. Then, from their lofty position of knowledge, the MBA-holders can counsel leaders in how to lead a business – but they have never run or led anything themselves.

The wise leader certainly will take advantage of the intellectual horsepower that these clever people can deliver, but she also will be very selective in the advice she takes.

If you are learning to ride a bicycle, you will only really trust a teacher who has actually ridden one and can demonstrate proficiency in the art. In contrast, a Physics PhD can explain to you on paper the theory of balance and velocity, but will fail to teach you to deal with the counter-intuitive ambiguities that cause the inevitable crash. Get a coach who can ride a bike.

And for your business leadership counsel, get a coach who has learned directly how to handle the ambiguities of SME leadership.

But, as with riding a bicycle, the only way to become really competent is to do it yourself and, through experience of what works, or more valuably what doesn't work, you will amass the vital experience required by every leader aspiring to deal with the ambiguities associated with an SME on its path of stellar growth.

5. Faces reality

Facing reality seems like an obvious response attitude for the deciding leader but, as with so much of life, the obvious is sometimes not so straightforward as it might appear. Despite their occasional aura of lofty self-assurance, leaders are human too and are thus subject to the fact that their responses are driven by what the evolutionary psychologists argue is the hardwiring of our brains to deal with the realities of Stone Age survival.

A primary, deep instinct for the survival of our ancestors 200,000 years ago was to put emotions before reason as the first screen for information. Feel fear – run – hide – wait.

Leadership of an SME, however, despite the hard-wiring of our brains and the undoubted fear that results from a serious competitive threat or internal crisis, demands that the leader does not run, does not hide, does not lie low. Deciding leaders must face reality without flinching, even though it goes against our incredibly powerful, basic evolutionary instincts.

Hiding from reality will not change anything, will not deal with the problem and certainly will not benefit the company, yet it is a reaction we have seen not only in others, but also in ourselves – to our considerable detriment. Lesson learned, we hope.

VISIONARY LEADER

Score yourself on each of the behaviours of the Visionary Leader below, using the following scoring range:

5 This is one of my outstanding characteristics. I demonstrate this much more than other leaders.

4 This is one of my key strengths. However, I think I could improve on my practice of this behaviour.

3 Sometimes I do this, but not often enough.

2 One of my weaker areas. I rarely demonstrate this. The behaviour does not sit well with me.

1 I don't use this behaviour and doubt if I could.

Total your score. The maximum score achievable is 100, so your score can be expressed as a percentage.

VISIONING		STRATEGISING	
Thinks entrepreneurially	☐	Sets ambitious goals	☐
Stretches boundaries	☐	Spots opportunities	☐
Dreams big dreams	☐	Plans methodically	☐
Thinks 'outside the box'	☐	Researches meticulously	☐
Bold in Vision	☐	Builds new concepts	☐

ENERGISING		DECIDING	
Inspires people	☐	Takes big risks	☐
Has high drive and ambition	☐	Takes hard decisions	☐
Demonstrates passion	☐	Tough-minded	☐
Very hard worker	☐	Handles ambiguity	☐
Looks to the future	☐	Faces reality	☐

Visionary Total %

Now transfer your score to page **206**.

5

THE TEAM–BUILDER LEADER

Team-builder leaders attract followers, mainly through the art of communication. They are strong believers in the value of collegiality, and are aware of the potential power available to the leader who can motivate individuals to participate in group activity towards the achievement of goals. Ernest Shackleton said:

> *There are many great things in the world … Comradeship is the best of them all.*

Team-building cannot work where there is insincerity, shallowness or selfishness. The superstar leader will have a genuine compassion for other people, recognising the problems they face from day to day as they wrestle with challenges and cope with opposition.

One of the coping mechanisms is for the leader to encourage a positive 'glass half-full' attitude for the entire team, and to create an environment where individuals feel strongly committed to the success of others within the team. Things don't always go well, even for the best ordered groups, but the team-builder will find a way to turn setbacks and failure to advantage, thus strengthening the group's confidence in themselves.

Also, of vital importance, a successful, confident team builds an aura of conquering power around the leader; all the members are infused with an identity of success through their association with this unique group and its talismanic leader.

It is like the true team spirit of the Emperor Napoleon's Old Guard, the US Green Berets, or the SAS. Bold in vision, careful in planning, ruthless in execution – but, of paramount importance, utterly loyal to the group, its values and its leader.

To establish such a spirit, the leader communicates openly, honestly and in regular, informal gatherings, so that individuals feel secure that they know where they are, in an organisation that operates with strict order and clear discipline.

While the precise, tightly-enforced, rigidities of military teams are neither present nor, indeed, appropriate in commercial SMEs, the broad principles still apply and are apparent in the selection, training and development of members and the removal of non-performers. There is no room for mediocrity in the high-performing top team, but it is not all about strictness and discipline.

The team-builder leader also ensures that his team has a comfortable working environment, again to underline the security that engenders confidence and enables the achievement of challenging goals.

Certainly, the leader sets eye-wateringly difficult challenges, but he matches chosen individuals to tasks for which they are suited. This leader knows his people well, knows their strengths, weaknesses, hopes, dreams, hurts and anxieties. All the time, as they strive towards their goals, the leader gives consistent, honest feedback and positive reward.

The team-builder leader is tolerant and kind. He uses 'tough love', with the frequent addition of engaging humour, to defuse the tensions that, inevitably, threaten to split high-performance teams.

The team know that mistakes will not condemn them to blame, provided they learn lessons from failure. They are comfortable with an environment that encourages them to let go of the past and to face reality fearlessly, avoiding an approach that will mire them in inertia.

The critical characteristics of the team-builder leader are:

- Demonstrable courage.
- Leading from the front.
- Communicable optimism.
- The ability to keep on going, when everyone else has exhausted the last dregs of their energy.

TEAM-BUILDER LEADERS –
THE DARK SIDE

If the core aim of the team-builder leader is to develop collegiality and teamwork through the creation of a powerful, directed culture, therein lies the hidden threat of malpractice. As a positive factor, culture can contribute differentiating competitive advantage to businesses of all sizes but, in the wrong hands, while employing all the positive features of team-building, it can be misused malignantly in a cynical, destructive orgy of wrongdoing.

The dark side is well-illustrated by the story of Jim and Tammy Bakker's PTL Club, an ostensibly evangelical Christian business. This enterprise employed all the elements of team-building leadership to build through mass communication a widespread culture of belonging for hundreds of thousands of people, many of them very poor. In due course, it became clear that these vulnerable searchers after fellowship were ripped off systematically, all the while believing they were part of a great and righteous crusade.

I n 1966, the Bakkers began working with Pat Robertson at his Christian Broadcasting Network, which at the time barely reached an audience of thousands. The Bakkers helped to drive the growth of the network, and their success with a variety show format, including interviews and puppets, helped to make *The 700 Club* one of the longest-running and most successful televangelism programmes.

The *Jim & Tammy Show* was aimed at young children, whom they entertained with such films as *Davey & Goliath*, a successful animation Bible-story series for children, which gave Jim and Tammy an initial launch-pad of popularity. The Bakkers left for California in the mid-1970s to team up with Paul and Jan Crouch.

The Crouchs and the Bakkers created the *Praise the Lord* show for the new Trinity Broadcasting Network in California and, while that relationship lasted only about a year, the Bakkers retained the rights to use the initials PTL. They then moved to Charlotte to begin their own show, *The PTL Club*.

Jim and Tammy's show, always focussing on family and group cultural identity, grew quickly, until it was carried by almost 100 stations, with average viewers numbering over 12 million. By this time, the business was growing rapidly and the Bakkers established their own network, the PTL Television Network. They are on record as attributing much of their success to decisions early on to accept all denominations and to refuse no one who would join their team – and give them money!

By the early 1980s, they had built Heritage USA, then the third most successful theme park in the US. They also hooked into a satellite system, to distribute their network 24 hours a day across the country. Contributions requested from viewers were estimated to exceed $1,000,000 a week, with proceeds intended to go to expanding the theme park and the team mission of PTL. But there was a sinister, dark side to Jim and Tammy's façade of team-building.

In their success, the Bakkers took personal conspicuous consumption to a bizarrely unusual level for a church-based non-profit organization. According to Frances FitzGerald of *The New Yorker*:

> *They epitomized the excesses of the 1980s; the greed, the love of glitz, and the shamelessness; which in their case was so pure as to almost amount to a kind of innocence.*

Despite all the outward show of crusading team-building, the 'kind of innocence' was ultimately exposed as a sham. Jim Bakker was involved in a sex scandal and the PTL organisation, which had built an amazing team constituency of followers, was revealed as financially fraudulent on a massive scale.

From 1984 to 1987, Bakker and his PTL associates had sold 'lifetime memberships' for $1,000 or more that entitled buyers to a three-night stay annually at a luxury hotel at the Heritage USA theme park. Bakker sold more 'exclusive' memberships than could be accommodated, while raising more than twice the money needed to build the actual hotel. According to the prosecution at Bakker's later fraud trial, tens of thousands of memberships had been sold, but only one 500-room hotel was ever completed.

A good deal of the money went into Heritage USA's operating expenses, while Bakker kept $3,700,000 for himself. To conceal the accounting irregularities, Bakker, who apparently made all of the financial decisions for the PTL organization, kept two sets of books.

Jerry Falwell, who took over the PTL Club after Jim Bakker's fall from grace, called him "a liar, an embezzler, a sexual deviant" and:

> "… the greatest scab and cancer on the face of Christianity in 2,000 years of church history".

Jim and Tammy Bakker stand as an example of when Team-building leadership becomes immoral manipulation.

Modern business literature and academic research rightly portrays the building of effective teams as one of the most important tasks facing the leader of a growing company. The character type, Team-builder leader, will display strong performance in four behavioural areas:

- Selecting.
- Communicating.
- Harmonising.
- Motivating.

SELECTING

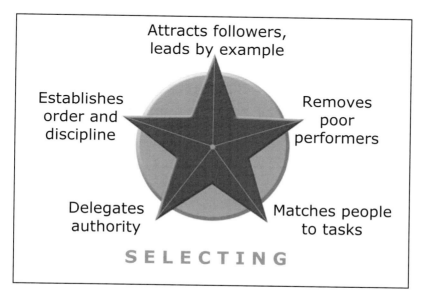

1. Attracts followers, leads by example

Before any selections can be carried out, it is fundamentally necessary to attract applicants or followers. It has been wryly commented that, if you are wondering whether you are a leader, all you have to do is take a look over your shoulder and see whether anybody is following.

Followers will be there for a variety of reasons. In most cases, in the SMEs and large corporations that we know, they are in the line simply out of economic necessity and the leaders are only kidding themselves that these wage-focussed individuals are followers in any real sense of the term.

The SME Team-builder leader will focus on attracting team aspirants who truly buy into the cause. From our experience of dealing with thousands of employees, we are of the firm view that the fundamental motivation for people at work is not money, but meaning. The most direct way for a leader to deliver meaning to followers is to lead by meaningful example: such delivery will attract managers and employees to participate in an exciting growth opportunity.

Attracting followers is easier if the leader has real charisma but, when this is allied to an obvious desire to lead from the front, then the key requirements for assembling a team of dedicated followers are in place.

When, for example, the business' success depends on regular grinding travel to far-off parts of the world, with all the attendant sacrifices of social and family life, and the leader is doing much more than her share, then those who see her example will be encouraged to follow the lead in all aspects of the company's development.

Anne Rutledge is a leader who is followed by a strong team. Today, Anne's eponymous international recruitment company attracts ambitious people who are prepared to travel the world, following Anne's intrepid entrepreneurial example in building her successful business from scratch.

An example from an earlier age is that of Ernest Shackleton, whose perilous expedition to Antarctica was highly over-subscribed, despite its obvious potential hardships and dangers. The hardy participants were attracted by Shackleton's vision, charisma, example and reputation.

2. Removes poor performers

Employment laws in Ireland and Britain make it very difficult to get rid of poor performers. In the interests of the company, its shareholders, its customers, its suppliers and, most important of all, the hard-working good performers, this is a task the selecting leader must not shirk.

Jack Welch famously attributed the success of GE to his policy of hiring and keeping only the best people, who he termed 'A's and 'B's and, by definition, ruthlessly getting rid of poor performers, who he termed 'C's. But this is easier to do in the US than in Europe, where employment legislation limits such action.

Since all companies are susceptible to global competition, it is arguable whether the restrictions on removing poor employees in Europe is in the long-term best interests either of the poor-performing individuals themselves, or of the companies who damage their competitiveness by carrying them.

In our view, however painful in the short term, it is also in the best interest of the poor performer that they be helped to move on to another opportunity that may suit their talents better. This is not a mere guilt-assuaging platitude. We mean it: take the case of Max.

T welve years ago at the beginning of the Internet age, we invested in a speculative entrepreneurial Internet venture with a staff of five skilled computer enthusiasts. One of them was a caricature of the extreme eccentricity often found among the supposed geeks and nerds who populate the industry.

Max had the requisite ponytail, was careless and bohemian in his clothes and overall lifestyle, but was highly skilled and pitched in with the rest to get the new business under way. The enthusiastic, well-led team expanded quickly over the next year, when things started to go awry with Max.

We couldn't get to the bottom of his problem, because he was virtually monosyllabic and not interested in discussion. But his work-quality deteriorated, his attendance was erratic and he was negatively affecting the performance of others who wanted to work hard.

We tried to sort him out but, at last, had to go through the statutory warning procedures, before finally terminating his employment. Some members of the team wanted to give Max more chances, but the CEO was insistent that he be removed as soon as employment law would permit. This was good leadership in action and the performance of both the team and the company quickly recovered after Max left.

He disappeared from our view for about a year, when he re-emerged as the technical director of a two-man start-up web media business. Within three years, it employed over 50 people and had attracted significant VC investment. One year later, it was sold to a major media player, turning Max, still complete with ponytail, into a millionaire.

3. Matches people to tasks

In the case above, removing a poor performer clearly lifted productivity, but leadership action in selecting the best and most suitable people for particular tasks within an SME will have even more dramatically-positive effects on outputs. To achieve such matching, it is obvious that the leader must be thoroughly aware of the strengths, weaknesses, goals and dreams of individuals, and must understand the nature and competency demands of the tasks involved.

Padraig McManus, as CEO of the ESB, Ireland's most profitable semi-State company, with a €4 billion turnover, certainly is not leading an SME, although, on reflection, despite the ESB's colossal overall size in the context of Irish enterprise, it is made up of many business units that could be described as SMEs. Padraig's approach to extracting top performance from his business carries exemplar lessons for the SME team-builder leader.

Padraig is a life-time career executive in ESB, with hands-on experience of the key tasks involved in building a world-class utility, but, in addition to his technical capability, he has the differentiating talent that turns a technocrat into a great team-builder leader. He is a 'people person'.

The bulk of Padraig's time is spent getting to know his people's capabilities and aspirations, so that he can ensure they are placed in the positions in the organisation where they can deliver most value.

Of course there is nothing new in such an approach. Many years ago, Will started his working life as an apprentice in a textile mill, where promising young people 'served their time' in different parts of the business. From spinning to weaving, to finishing the cloth, on to clothing manufacture and, ultimately, to selling to wholesalers or retailers, both home and export.

Throughout the process, the apprentices were monitored and mentored, leading to an assessment of where their skills could be best applied in their future career of service to the firm. Happy days for Will, who, his sales talents matched to his future task, finished the apprenticeship in export sales in the USA and Europe.

4. Delegates authority

It is perhaps in the area of delegation of authority that SME Team-builder leaders can learn most from best practice, as applied within major corporations. Here, the immense complexity of tasks and relationships, together with the variables associated with managing huge numbers of people, mean that there is simply no other way to lead than to delegate effectively.

The career executives who have spent their working lives in that environment are also well-attuned to a culture of hierarchical authority and 'division of labour' in the achievement of objectives.

An autocratic SME leader can get away with holding back on delegation for a time, while the company's ambitions are small, maybe even for quite a long time, but, if there is a will to grow, then delegation of authority is unavoidable and the autocrat must change or hand over to someone who can – and will – delegate.

M ark Sweeney is CEO of the 3,000-strong FG Wilson engineering business in Northern Ireland. Under the early leadership of the visionary innovator-founder, Fred Wilson, and his family, this company had grown from nothing to a point where it was a world-wide competitor in the manufacture of generating sets. Its success made it an attractive takeover candidate for the giant Caterpillar Group.

Mark has streamlined the business with a strategy of developing a strong cadre of managers, to whom he has delegated the authority, and also the broad autonomy, to run the main functional areas of the business. The key to success in his process is to select managers with the right attitude, train them well, match them to the right tasks and then lead the balanced team.

Mark Sweeney is running a very large company, but his approach to delegation is directly applicable to every SME.

5. Establishes order and discipline

An undisciplined and disorganised team will find it very difficult to compete with an ordered, disciplined group, regardless of the individual talents of its members.

Roy Keane's comment on the performance of the England soccer team, when they failed to qualify for the European finals in 2008, essentially was that they failed because, while the team had players with sufficient ability, they were not playing as an organised team and they did not appear to be fully committed to the cause.

Staying with the football analogy, there is no explanation why a team like Northern Ireland, made up of less-talented individual players from lowly divisions, can hold their own with the cream of the Premiership and Europe, other than that they are better ordered and better disciplined than their rivals.

O rder and discipline is a high priority for the board of an SME such as Chambers, the leading private sector competitor to the public sector-owned Translink transport giant in Northern Ireland. The highly-experienced chairman, Ted Hesketh, steers with a firm and steady hand, driving the culture from the top down in an ordered and disciplined way. Roles are clear, expectation levels challenging, and accountability absolute at board, management and employee levels.

The first rule of success for an SME towards the establishment of competitive advantage in this area is the appointment of an effective chairman to a highly-competent, well-balanced board of directors.

The managing director who is accountable to such a body will ensure that a culture of good order is established, to mirror that of the board, and will impose appropriate disciplines on the operation of the company. The main positive outcome from all this order is that employees, managers and directors feel, above all, that they are secure and, hence, the team will operate as a cohesive and competitive group.

COMMUNICATING

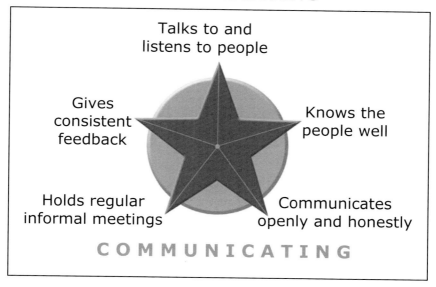

Communication is the oil that lubricates the machinery of the team, to keep it running smoothly. While it forces us to mix metaphors, it is also the glue that sticks the team together, in the face of forces that would break it up. If the team leadership does not communicate, neither will the team; if the team does not communicate, it will not function, nor will it be sustainable as a competitive entity.

The Team-builder leader has a vital role in imposing, or encouraging, a culture of easy engagement between team members, forbidding the formation of cliques and silos.

1. Talks to and listens to people

The measure of whether a CEO is fulfilling the Team-builder role through communication leadership is a function of the degree and quality of their conversations with, and their listening to, the team. Naturally, part of the contact value is simply down to time spent, but more important is the empathy, engagement and even emotion of the dialogue.

J ohn Maguire is CEO of the world-famous Belleek pottery in County Fermanagh, where Parian china has been manufactured for international markets for almost 200 years. John is a Fermanagh man himself, who joined the company after his university education and was promoted through the ranks as a result of his diligence, insightful management ability and perceptive communication skills.

By the time he arrived in the top job, Belleek was ready for change – in more ways than one. The buildings and facilities were in need of major overhaul, systems and processes were outmoded, product ranges were dull and markets were shrinking. In short, the company whose china had graced the tables of European royalty, enhanced the decoration of American mansions, and provided a tangible link with home for the Irish diaspora was tired and old; but it still had a loyal, highly-skilled workforce. It needed rejuvenation, and the young, energetic John Maguire, backed fully by the owner, Dr George Moore, was just the man for the job.

Buildings, systems, product ranges and market development all can be changed for the better by capital investment, and George courageously invested, but the real turnaround came about due to the mind-changes inspired through John Maguire's tireless communication with his strong top team and the loyal workforce. He listened carefully to his staff's suggestions and concerns and explained the vision for the future.

The renewed company grew organically and, by the acquisition of Galway Crystal, Aynsley China and Donegal Parian China, now has reached a turnover in excess of £20 million. Belleek struggling became Belleek Living – the name of its latest sophisticated product group. John Maguire is the communicating leader who built and led this transformational team.

2. Knows the people well

Sometimes the best means of demonstrating the correct way to carry out a task or process is to show a situation where the particular activity is being done badly – and then recommend that the opposite approach is taken.

Knowing people well is not as easy as it sounds or looks and faking it is a trap for the insincere, or hypocritical, pretender. For obvious reasons, the identities of the 'hero' of this story and his company are disguised.

George is a very wealthy, self-made 45-year-old owner of a group of Irish companies involved in IT and property development, seemingly with a Midas touch. He is also a courteous, well-meaning person and, as a client, is easy to work with, though he tends to show off and to attract attention to himself. Most of his time is spent flitting from one business to another, doing deals, or flying to London, New York or Budapest in search of a new opportunity. He has three MDs who run the day-to-day operations of his empire, so he himself does not take much time to talk directly to the people he employs.

Last year, in an attempt to increase contact with his people, and accompanied by us, he made a formal visit to each business unit. At the first site, he addressed the staff with a speech on how the Group was trading. All fair enough, so far – but then George blew it.

When he had finished the scripted trading update, he started into a session of false bonhomie and familiarity with people whom he hardly knows. He got names wrong, used nicknames, told inappropriate laddish jokes – the embarrassment was palpably obvious to everyone, except George, who thought he had put on a wonderful bonding performance.

As one young woman remarked at the post-meeting reception:

> *"Now I know what it's like to work with David Brent!".*

The following morning's de-briefing, when we told George the truth, brought an angry, hurt response and almost ended our business relationship, but we had to ensure that he did not compound his earlier gaffe by repeating the performance at the next two meetings. When the emotion died down, George accepted his mistake.

We coached him on his core presentation and, in the second and third meetings, George was sincere, with no pretence of familiarity, and just showed his natural, courteous self. These meetings were a great success, with no mention of David Brent or *The Office* afterwards.

Knowing people well takes a large investment of time and, most of all, demands total sincerity. George isn't there yet, but he's working on the critical issue for a communicating leader – getting to know more people in his business.

3. Communicates openly and honestly

Openness and honesty are vital hallmarks of sincerity in all walks of life and, while they are clearly important for the communicating SME leader, they are by no means universally evident in commercial life. The reason simply is that both characteristics leave the leader vulnerable to attack from those with more devious motives. It takes a high degree of self-confidence to cope with voluntarily inviting such potential threats.

The upside, however, is that there is no better way to build a reputation for straight-dealing than to expose the vulnerable flank and be prepared to take the attendant risks. Very few SMEs get through their growth history without hitting severe financial, market or competitive pressures along the way. It is at such times that the temptation to hide and, paradoxically, the need for openness and honesty is greatest.

T his real vulnerability is illustrated by the experience of Michael Holt's £10 million distribution business, when he lost a major supplier, just after he had spent £600,000 installing automated picking technology in a part of the business that was showing strong growth.

In keeping with Michael's policy of open information, earlier he had informed his workforce of the potential benefits of the new investment and how not only would it make their lives easier, but how the growth would lead to expansion and an increase in employment.

Naturally, everyone was excited – and then came the unexpected bombshell: the news that a multi-national supplier of Holt was moving into the market with a direct salesforce and Holt Logistics would lose £2,500,000 of turnover within six months, a third of it disappearing right away.

When he received the news, Michael was devastated, because it came without warning and his financial director could not see in the long-term how the business could support its fixed costs on the basis of such a dramatically-reduced contribution. In addition, a greater short-term threat loomed, in that the recent capital investment had impacted severely on Holt's liquidity, and so the company faced a catastrophic cash crisis.

Michael told us frankly that his first terror-induced reaction was to cover up, put on a brave face and pretend everything was going to be OK but, on brief reflection, he did not take this course of action. He banked on his past reputation for openness and integrity and went for open disclosure.

First, he told his workforce, which was painful in the extreme, as at the same time he had to make 12 people redundant, 8 of whom had served the company loyally since its formation 15 years earlier. Despite his openness and honesty, Michael didn't win any prizes in those discussions.

Then he spoke to his other suppliers, with whom he had dealt in a transparent and open relationship for years, and asked them to give him an extra month's credit for the next nine month's trading. That was agreed and took care of the medium-term cash crisis.

Finally, and within four days of receiving the bad news, he met his bank, which on the basis of his past open dealings backed him with additional funds to cover the immediate shortfall.

Michael Holt's reputation for trust, and his swift implementation of open, honest communication, saved his company, saved 47 jobs and, in the face of slashing the size of his team, demonstrated courageous team-building leadership of the highest order. Today, four years later, his growing SME employs 82 people.

4. Holds regular informal meetings

Twenty-five years ago, Tom Peters and Bob Waterman coined the phrase 'management by walking around' (MBWA), in their ground-breaking classic *In Search of Excellence*.[16] At that time, it seemed a much more revolutionary concept than perhaps it does today, as in the intervening period their idea almost has become accepted practice for any business leader.

The essence of the approach is that the leader should be very visible, physically present and available for interaction with other members of the senior team and, indeed, the entire company. But its power is derived from a more than mere availability: it comes from the positive team-building effect of the leader taking a genuine, knowledgeable interest in what employees are doing in their daily work. The contact must be regular, it must be easy and informal, and the right people must be involved at the right time.

We know many SME leaders who, like Derek McCracken when he was interim chief executive of Adamsez, the high-profile bath manufacturer, make their first action on arriving at the plant early in the morning an informal walk-around. They take a varying route, stopping to ask people how things are going with their section, pulling together two or three operatives to discuss a current problem and moving on quickly, in order to keep a sense of urgency.

---

[16]   Thomas J. Peters & Robert H. Waterman, *In Search of Excellence: Lessons from America's Best-run Companies*, HarperBusiness, 1982.

There is no false *bonhomie* with Derek's approach, no lengthy gossip about last night's football match, though it may be referred to briefly before getting down to business. Because it is handled with this friendly, open, informal but businesslike breeziness, people feel comfortable in stopping Derek if they need to, or letting him walk on by with a nod if the need is not there.

All well-run companies will have their regular formal meetings, but the leaders of SMEs that truly are 'in search of excellence' will also make sure that informality and regularity are a feature of contact at all levels of the business.

5. Gives consistent feedback

In his robust model for assessing the strength of a company's strategy, Michael Porter lists 'continuity and consistency' as one of five key attributes of strategic integrity.[17] When it comes to assessing the communication effectiveness of a Team-builder leader, we do not need to look beyond the advice of this great Harvard Business School guru.

But consistency is not enough, if it is consistency of reticence or silence. The consistency of communication that adds team-building value is laden with learning content and, through its regularity, causes no surprises to the recipients – whether it be teaching, encouragement, congratulation or rebuke.

T om Sands is a mercurial, hard-driving MD of a 35-strong Scottish training consultancy. He is an engaging public speaker, an excellent teacher and has helped hundreds of business executives and sales people to improve their performance. But he has a flaw that results in his otherwise well-run business experiencing a much higher level of employee turnover than its competitors; his weakness is related to inconsistency in the manner and content of feedback to his own staff of consultants and trainers.

---

[17]   Michael E. Porter, *Competitive Advantage: Creating & Sustaining Superior Performance*, The Free Press, 1985.

Tom can be the life and soul of the party, or Tom can be sullen and moody. There is not much in between. The added difficulty for his staff is that there is no way of knowing at any particular time which frame of mind he will be in and whether their discussion will be conducted with friendly, upbeat jocularity, or menacing black depression. Either way, they are treading on eggshells and have to endure the tension of highly-inconsistent behaviour.

A contrast can be found in the approach of Kevin Quigley, COO of Garage Door Systems, a chartered accountant by training. In common with many people from this background, Kevin is steady, unflappable and driven by facts. The type of feedback he delivers is consistent in manner and content and provides the recipients with value-adding teaching motivation or direct criticism, as appropriate.

His demeanour also is shaped consistently by the content of the situational discussion. His staff do not get surprises when they are counselled with a smile, or a joke if their performance is good, or when they are roundly chastised if their performance is bad. Kevin is no soft touch, and staff can wilt under his forensic questioning, but he is remorselessly consistent and thus is respected by all his people.

A striking difference between Tom and Kevin in terms of communication consistency in the delivery of feedback is that Tom is highly likely to bawl out the carrier of bad news – Kevin will never shoot the messenger.

HARMONISING

The top team in a rapidly growing SME is subject to daily pressures, some of which, because of their inherent challenge are positive in terms of teambuilding effect. Some however are negative, setting one individual or function against another, while others are deeply malignant and can threaten the total survival of genuine team ethos within the group.

The pressures may be caused by external competitive events, internal politics, functional rivalries or private and personal hurts;

but the Team-builder leader must keep a weather-eye open for disruptive threats to team unity that require the intervention of harmonising leadership.

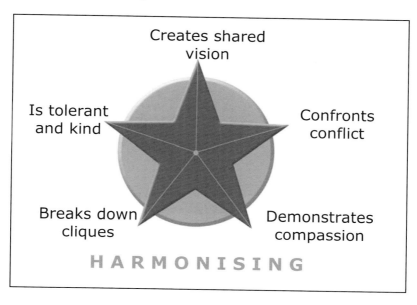

1. Creates shared vision

The active creation of shared vision or common purpose arguably is the most important contribution to business success of any SME team leader. This is the alchemy that takes elements of individually rich talents or characteristics and blends the complex mix into a form of infinitely greater value than the sum of all its parts.

William Grant & Sons Ltd has been manufacturing Scotch whisky over five generations. Its leading brands, including *Glenfiddich* and *Grant's*, are famous throughout the world. It is a large company and not an SME by any stretch of the imagination, but it belongs in this book because, unlike the global giants with which it competes successfully, Grant's is still a family business, still exhibiting the entrepreneurial traits of its founder, William Grant.

Recently, we spent a day with fifth-generation family members, cousins Grant and Peter Gordon, at the vast 220-acre William Grant distilling complex in Girvan, Scotland. During this fascinating visit, we saw every aspect of the process and met many of the personnel engaged in turning out these finest of whiskies.

We saw a huge business, with hundreds of millions of pounds invested in stock, capital equipment and brand development, but where all of the staff exhibited the same level of enthusiasm, passion and commitment to excellence so clearly evident in the values held by the current progeny of William Grant.

The clinical professionalism of the staff and their easy familiarity with both Peter and Grant Gordon demonstrates the shared values and vision alignment of front-line people with the directors and corporate shareholders. Such rapport is rarely seen in SMEs, never mind a massive company like William Grant, with millions of pounds of global branded sales.

2. Confronts conflict

Leaders with the confidence to recognise the positive benefits of creative conflict will orchestrate a healthy crackling tension of challenge for growth-achieving individuals and teams. Such dynamic leadership is more commonly found in start-ups or rapidly growing SMEs than in large corporations but, recently, we met with the CEO of a major company who is one of the exceptions that proves the rule.

T hrough brave investment, at a time when few were investing in Ireland, the entrepreneurial Roche family established and grew NTR from small beginnings to become an Irish superstar company. For the next stage of growth, in 2000, they brought 33-year-old Jim Barry on board.

Jim is a charismatic, straight-talking CEO with the hallmark sophisticated presence and bearing of a classically-educated, internationally-experienced, corporate superstar. Graduating from the Harvard Business School, he spent four years as a consultant with cutting-edge consultants Bain & Company and then worked on international mergers and acquisitions with Morgan Stanley.

Will introduced the discussion on internal conflict in businesses by commenting that, obviously, NTR is not a small company and thus perhaps the dynamics are different to those in an SME. He was brought up sharply by Jim's insistence that NTR started as an SME.

Apart from a few acquisitions, most of its growth is fuelled by the establishment of start-ups, followed by their early-stage expansion, then development and growth and onto the mature growth stage. At this point, NTR may take an exit, as in its phenomenally successful sale of Airtricity in 2007.

Jim Barry's way of managing the negative and positive dimensions of conflict is first to establish the clarity and integrity of the operating process; then he does not interfere, provided there is no corruption of that design. Through pre-emptive design, he creates robust alignment and, within an entrepreneurial culture founded on integrity, the team itself then demands the highest standards of performance of its people.

This is not a cosy environment where conflict is ignored, as Jim's comments indicate:

> *"Conflict, positive or negative must be faced head on – and quickly. Messengers bringing bad news don't get shot. Non-communicators will get shot".*

While at first glance, this unequivocally-direct attitude appears to strike a discordant note with the harmonising behaviour demanded of the Team-builder leader, we are convinced it is a key contributor to positive team dynamics. Its directness means that people feel secure, confident and know clearly what is expected of them.

3. Demonstrates compassion

The macho business creed of competitiveness that regards every transaction as a zero-sum game, that portrays competitors as the sworn enemy, that assumes buyers and sellers are out to rape each other and boasts that the winner takes it all, would not have sat comfortably with the Quaker business families of the 18th and 19th centuries.

Through their faith-driven reputation for absolute honesty, this small sect owned and controlled Irish and British commercial interests out of all proportion to their numbers. The discrimination that kept them out of the professions drove them to trade with each other and, on the back of their demonstrable success and integrity, outsiders sought them out as business associates or trading partners, thus enabling the growth of dynasties, such as the Richardson and La Touche families in Ireland and the Cadburys and Frys in England.

The Quakers enabled trade in those early days, because it was possible for a trader partner to know that transactions could be made quickly and surely, on the basis of 'my word is my bond'. This, together with the Quakers' meticulous adherence to accurate bookkeeping, also gave comfort that payment terms would be honoured scrupulously.

Those who worked in the Quaker enterprises of the formative years of Western capitalism were intensely loyal, hardworking, and collaborative employees, due to the harmonising effects of relatively-benign working conditions. These early team-building employers showed genuine compassion for the people who worked for them, as an outward expression of their faith, which also impelled them to the forefront of the great, but initially very unpopular, humanitarian movement to abolish slavery.

This compassion for workers, while its roots were wholly altruistic and not motivated by the prospect of financial gain, quickly resulted in a team-based, productivity-led competitive advantage, making the Quakers yet more prosperous; no doubt, they ascribed their good fortune to the righteous beneficence of their God. Their commercial success, on the back of enlightened compassion, is a clear example to the SME team-building leader of the 21st century.

4. Breaks down cliques

While one aspect of sustainable team-building concerns the pro-active assembling of synergistic talents and blending them to create a powerful means of achieving a desired goal, another is to actively avoid the fragmentation of a functioning group.

Internal struggles for power, or straightforward personal jealousies, can break the best of alliances and the harmonising leader will watch carefully for any emerging signs of dissonance. In our experience, both with SMEs and large corporations, cliques form given certain situational and cultural conditions:

- They have a leader with an agenda, which may have little benefit for the other members of the clique, although he will manipulate them skilfully to ensure that their weight is thrown behind him in pursuance of his own ends.

- The clique can fester and grow where people are under-employed and have time on their hands, in which to develop the malevolent activity of their group – as the proverb says, 'The devil makes mischief for idle hands'.

- Where a group is not given a clear understanding of their goal, then sub-groups are prone to form and visualise their own goals, which are likely to diverge from the SME leader's goals.

On the first signs of factionalism, the SME leader should act as advised by Jim Barry of NTR earlier: face the issue directly, do it speedily, clarify goals and alignment, and squarely face both non-communicators and the non-compliant who do not buy into the team ethos.

5. Is tolerant and kind

Business leadership in the 1980s and 1990s often followed the ruthless, rapacious, 'greed is good' attitude of the Gordon Gekko Wall Street character, and it didn't only happen in fiction. Books such as *Barbarians at the Gate*[18] and *Greed & Glory on Wall Street*[19] graphically describe the true stories of self-interest and downright cruelty that ultimately brought colossal financial empires like Lehman Brothers to their knees.

---

[18] Bryan Burrough & John Helyar, *Barbarians at the Gate: The Fall of RJR Nabisco*, HarperPerennial, 1992.

[19] Ken Auletta, *Greed & Glory on Wall Street: The Fall of the House of Lehman*, Random House, 1986.

Harsh, tough, uncaring leaders still have their supporters, and many investors have seen their personal wealth greatly enhanced by backing them, but the collapses written about in these two books and the later scandals of WorldCom, Tyco and Enron, raise serious questions about hard leadership.

Recently, widespread research of softer, kinder, quieter leadership styles, as described by Joseph Badaracco in *Leading Quietly*,[20] have underlined what the harmonising SME Team-builder knew all along – that empathy, encouragement and sympathetic support for individuals, as they strive to fulfil challenging tasks, will imbue a team with momentum that no slavishly- or cruelly-driven group can be impelled to match.

The enlightened harmoniser will impose zero tolerance of carelessness, laziness or bad workmanship, but will allow great tolerance of genuine mistakes, or even sub-standard performance, where there is a desire to improve and to learn. This leader will always look for the opportunity to perform small acts of kindness to ease the lot of her people, as they encounter the inevitable hurts and setbacks of life.

Enlightened harmonisers do not act kindly so that they can be seen; word gets out, but whether seen or unseen, kindness always has its reward. Many SMEs in Ireland and Britain actively support voluntary humanitarian aid projects worldwide and the team-building benefit of such efforts is immense, because people feel individually involved as part of the corporate kindness.

W e heard of an interesting slant on this in an Australian SME that was suffering from absenteeism, although the leader had tried a number of financial incentive schemes to correct it, but without success. Then he had the innovative – and kind – idea for the company to charitably fund an orphanage each month, up to a certain generous amount.

If there was no absenteeism, the contribution would be paid to the orphanage in full but, for every absentee day, it would be reduced

---

[20]   Joseph Badaracco, *Leading Quietly: An Unorthodox Guide to Doing the Right Thing*, Harvard Business School Press, 2002.

by a stated amount. Financially, it made absolutely no difference to the employees, yet following the introduction of the scheme, absenteeism dropped to a negligible level.

Responsible kindness in action by a leader can have life-changing consequences for those who benefit from its effects, or observe it in action. We love this true story recently broadcast by BBC Northern Ireland, where a 70-year old lady from rural Ireland was reminiscing on a moment in time and an act of kindness that inspired her as a nine-year-old child:

We always were sent to Confession on Saturday. For some reason, I was on my own that day and I went into Confession and when I came out again the sky was very overcast, and I just got down past the beautiful thatched house called Farthings, *when the skies opened and the rain came dashin' down. And you couldn't shelter, if it was thunder and lightning you couldn't shelter under trees and that was all the shelter there was, so I began to run down the road. And I was coming past Greenfields Estate and the door of the gate lodge was opened and a lady was standing at the door. And she said to me, "Come on in, wee McCallion", she said, "you will be drooped to the skin, you can wait here until the rain goes over".*

And she brought me in. And I went into the house and the house was like a furnace because the big range was on and she was baking. And there was a baby in a big pram, rocking away. She brought me over to the fire to sit in the chair – it was just an ordinary kitchen chair, and she said to me, "Sit down there by the fire until you get yourself dried". It was a big black range with a rack above it.

She took my shoes and socks off and she dried my feet and she hung my socks up over the rack of the stove, and she took the bow off my hair and she dried my hair with a towel and then she combed it, and by the time she did that the ribbon was dry. She put it back in my hair and she tied it. Oh … she was just … the loveliest woman you could ever imagine!

She had one of those crossover flowery aprons on her and she had dimples on her elbows as she worked the dough in the bowl. And she was very pretty, very, very pretty and plump, not fat, plump. And every so often, she would just brush her hair back like that there and so she had a piece of flour on her face.

As I was sitting in the kitchen, there was a wire, a couple of wire trays and on them there were these lovely wee jam tarts and the smell was scrumptious. She said to me, "Would you like a wee drop of milk?", and I said, "Yes, please". She brought this milk out in a lovely wee flowery cup. And then she gave me, not one, but two jam tarts. Now this was the war and one jam tart was a luxury but two jam tarts were riches beyond treasure. And I never had two jam tarts to myself. Usually, it was a half – they were always divided up. But I sat, and I … I was in heaven. And they were the most delicious jam tarts. Lovely and crumbly and buttery and the jam was as sweet as honey. Beautiful. They were a real treat. A real treat to me. My mother would have baked you know, treacle bread and fadge, and those kind of things, you know … sensible things.

Whenever the rain went over, or ceased a bit anyway, she put four jam tarts in a blue sugar bag and she gave them to me to take home to the rest. And I went down the road and I thought I was in heaven. And I said to myself, "When I grow up, I am going to be kind and good and lovely like Mrs. King".

MOTIVATING

Skills and techniques of motivation are a fundamentally important team-building focus of sports coaches, politicians, schoolteachers, business managers and team leaders, in every team-based competitive activity or organisation. True teams are absent, if there is no team-building; team-building is absent, if there is no leadership; leadership is absent, if there is no leading; leading is absent, if there is no motivation.

This critical significance in the chain of team creation means that the quality of implemented motivation can make or break a team's chances of success. It has many important characteristics, five of which are crucial.

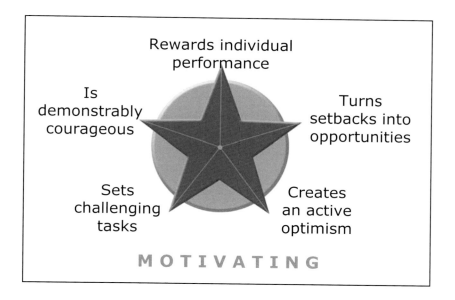

1. Rewards individual performance

Teams, by definition, are collections of individuals and while, in theory, an overall group reward should be enough to motivate all the participants to optimise their delivery effort, in practice it has been well-documented that a mixture of team and individual rewards is the better approach.

M anchester United, as one of the top teams in the English Premiership, wins most of its matches but, even when winning, the manager, Sir Alex Ferguson, frequently will substitute players during a game. Some of these substitutions are tactical and the players will not be overly dismayed at being replaced, but many of the substitutions are simply because the player is not performing to the level required by Sir Alex.

World-class professional footballers are very proud, extremely wealthy young men, often with the demeanour and self-regard of prima donnas. They hate the experience of being substituted, which holds them up to the fans as under-performers. The motivating target that drives them is to be in the starting 11 and to see the game through to the end, having performed well enough to stay on the pitch.

A leader who has the level of respect enjoyed by Sir Alex can deliver match-winning motivation to a player by a few words from the touchline. Footballers are also rewarded financially, in direct correlation to the success of their efforts on the field. The joint effect of the encouraging word, together with the money in the bank, is the formula used in winning clubs.

It is no different in principle in a stellar-growth SME, where the team can be rewarded overall, but it is in singling out individuals in recognition of special effort or achievement that motivation has its greatest effect.

The most difficult aspect of the process of rewarding on a one-on-one basis is having to make the choices on individuals who will not be rewarded, due to lower than best performance. Some people must be left out, or the entire motivational effect is lost. It is essential that there is sufficient differentiation in reward, between those who profit and those who do not, for the winners to feel special and for the 'losers' to identify clearly the standards they must reach, in order to be the winners of the future.

2. Turns setbacks into opportunities

Nothing a leader does motivates a team as much as displaying the leadership, which when the group has suffered a hit, by the use of initiative, intelligence, native wit or sheer panache, turns the reverse in fortune into a positive opportunity.

Harland Sanders started his working life as a poor farmhand and struggled financially until his middle age, when he took an old family recipe for fried chicken and built a modest, but reasonably prosperous, business.

His early enterprise provided for himself, his family and a small team of employees. This single-site dream business was his pride and joy but, after seven years' trading, the property burned to the ground and he had to start again.

He and his small team did not give up and got going again but, after further years of struggle, disaster struck again, when the highway was re-routed. His trade disappeared and, once more, Harland Sanders had to close down his business.

By this time, Harland was 66 years old and broke but, with intelligent initiative and panache, he announced himself to the world as 'Colonel' Sanders and launched his new 'finger-lickin' good' chicken business as a franchising model.

Within four years, Sanders had sold his Kentucky Fried Chicken concept to 400 restaurants in the Southern States.

Out of setbacks that would have destroyed much younger men, he motivated and led his team to create an opportunity, which became the largest take-out chicken business in the world. He had the resilience to cope with disappointment and the breadth of vision to look forward to new opportunities.

Through motivational leadership, Harland Sanders' franchise model inspired thousands of people to overcome setbacks and to find opportunities for commercial success.

'Colonel' Sanders sold the name, but remained the iconic leader of his creation until he died a wealthy and contented man at the venerable age of 90.

3. Creates an active optimism

Norman Kilroy, former managing director of Grafton Group plc and a former chairman of the Irish Management Institute, is quoted as saying that:

"… enthusiasm is the most important leadership quality".

Enthusiasm is highly infectious and this successful business personality refers to a common trait among great leaders, such as Martin Luther King, John F Kennedy, Nelson Mandela and even Big Jack Charlton, which is their ability to identify enthusiastically with the needs and aspirations of their followers.

Team-building leaders who create a positive optimism can improve their own performance greatly, as well as that of the team, and also enhance company growth prospects. Sports coaches are aware of the power of positive thinking, which is why the pre-match team talk has such importance in every club game, league contest, cup final and international test match.

One of the earliest proponents of the effectiveness of this attitude was another Norman, Norman Vincent Peale, who wrote *The Power of Positive Thinking*[21] in 1952. While its basic thoughts were set within the frame of the Reverend Peale's Methodism, modern literature on the subject borrows heavily from his argument that positivity is largely a matter of choice for the individual or group. The leader who can present this idea convincingly can change the competitive aspirations of a team, while increasing its bonding.

To create an active optimism, a team-builder leader must say the right words confidently, must speak empathetically in the right tones, must demonstrate clearly a positive example and must lead the SME team emphatically from the front.

4. Sets challenging tasks

Motivation is generally poor in organisations where expectations are set at a low level and where there is little urgency or challenge. It is a feature of the human spirit that, where a severe challenge, or even life-threatening danger, exists, the purposeful overcoming of adversity is a factor of immense motivating power.

I n the late 1960s, at the beginning of Will's business career, when he worked as a textile salesman in Europe, his sales director Graham Hudspith occasionally accompanied him on trips. On one weekend, during a selling tour to Belgium, Northern France and Germany, they visited a war cemetery where thousands of Allied casualties of World War II were buried.

Just over 20 years earlier, Mr Hudspith had been a Major in a British tank regiment, supporting the American troops facing the German Panzer divisions in the Battle of the Bulge, towards the end of the war.

He and Will walked through the rows and rows of white headstones, until they stopped at the one Mr Hudspith was looking for – the grave of his best friend, Charles.

---

[21] Norman Vincent Peale, *The Power of Positive Thinking*, Prentice-Hall, 1952.

Mr Hudspith told Will the story of how they were given the challenge of taking a fortified railway station and, after the tanks had broken through the lines of defence, he and his friend were leading a small group of soldiers on foot into the station complex, to ensure that resistance had been overcome fully.

His friend was immediately in front of him as they came to the corner of a building. As Charles looked carefully round the corner to check that all was clear, Mr Hudspith heard the crack of a rifle and his friend fell dead at his feet, shot in the head.

Will, moved by the story and having no experience of war, asked about the fear, the challenges and the motivation to keep on going in the face of such traumatic, yet commonplace, incidents. The reply was completely unexpected:

> *"I felt real sickening fear; but the adrenalin rush from the challenges was intense and, to be honest, I have never been so motivated since. They were the happiest days of my life".*

We live in softer, easier times, but the team-builder leader still can use onerous, demanding challenge to good effect in motivating the individuals in an SME top team.

5. Is demonstrably courageous

Courage in the face of threat or danger is a highly-infectious motivator, but its demonstration is not through shallow bravado or impetuosity, both of which are likely to be interpreted as rashness.

In business, the opportunities to demonstrate courage may be limited but, from time to time, such situations do arise and resilient bravery becomes visible.

Some years ago, we were involved in an SME that required a high level of upfront investment, with consequent high borrowings, in order to bring the product to market. Just before the business started to generate any income, the MD took seriously ill and could no longer participate.

As a result, there was an immediate loss of confidence by the company's banks, investors, employees and other stakeholders. The company almost collapsed under its weight of debt and external competitive threats. It was saved by the courageous leadership of the MD's son and his small dedicated team.

The MD was Will and the son was John. While he was recovering his strength, Will was completely oblivious of the stresses and pressures faced by John, in his lonely task of building the recovery of the business.

After it was all over and things were back on an even keel, Will asked John how he had had the courage to cope with the many black, troublesome, anxious days:

> *"Well, Will, it did initially hit me very hard and I honestly thought we would not make it. I felt like I was drowning and I was losing the will to struggle on. Then, one night, I was watching the* Discovery *channel on TV and I saw a documentary about a wee 12-year-old Indian orphan, who lived literally on a refuse tip outside Calcutta. He was blind, had only one arm and he spent his time scavenging in the rubbish to get enough to eat.*

> *And, as I sat in my comfortable chair and reflected on my comparative good fortune, I thought to myself, 'That wee boy would gladly exchange all the rest of his life for just one of my worst days'".*

Every day that John went into work during those stressful times, his team were watching him, to draw strength from his courage. He could not afford to show weakness in the face of pressure, or their motivation would have been weakened and the company's future imperilled.

John stayed strong, the team stayed strong and, in due time, their courage was rewarded by the company's success.

TEAM-BUILDER LEADER

Score yourself on each of the behaviours of the Team-builder Leader below, using the following scoring range:

5 This is one of my outstanding characteristics. I demonstrate this much more than other leaders.

4 This is one of my key strengths. However, I think I could improve on my practice of this behaviour.

3 Sometimes I do this, but not often enough.

2 One of my weaker areas. I rarely demonstrate this. The behaviour does not sit well with me.

1 I don't use this behaviour and doubt if I could.

Total your score. The maximum score achievable is 100, so your score can be expressed as a percentage.

SELECTING

Attracts followers, leads by example ☐

Removes poor followers ☐

Matches people to tasks ☐

Delegates authority ☐

Establishes order and discipline ☐

COMMUNICATING

Talks, and listens, to people ☐

Knows the people well ☐

Communicates openly / honestly ☐

Holds regular informal meetings ☐

Gives consistent feedback ☐

HARMONISING

Creates shared vision ☐

Confronts conflict ☐

Demonstrates compassion ☐

Breaks down cliques ☐

Is tolerant and kind ☐

MOTIVATING

Rewards individual performances ☐

Turns setbacks into opportunities ☐

Creates a positive optimism ☐

Sets challenging tasks ☐

Is demonstrably courageous ☐

Team-builder Total % ☐

Now transfer your scores to page **206**.

6

THE SELLER LEADER

Dr John King is one of Ireland's leading entrepreneurs, having led the pharmaceutical company Galen from its early stage as an SME, through a successful IPO, to the ultimate acquisition of Warner Chilcott in the US. In a speech delivered to Northern Ireland's top business-people at the Culloden Hotel, Belfast, John summed up his thoughts on commercial success by emphasising that continuing focus on the selling function is of prime importance in any company's range of priorities.

With John King's track record of having grown a small business to international prominence, propelling him and his colleague, Allen McClay, to the upper reaches of *The Sunday Times* 'Rich List', this nugget of advice is well worth hearing by all SME leaders.

The Seller leader's route to success is different from that of the visionary entrepreneur. Sellers are tremendous networkers, with great empathy for people. They want to create solutions for their customers, to develop their employees, and generally to assist colleagues and everyone with whom they come in contact. They are highly-effective social animals and greatly increase the currency value of contacts, both inside and outside the enterprise.

People want to do business with Seller leaders. These individuals are convinced of, and fully committed to, the key importance of selling and they will invest in, train, motivate and support their sales-force and individual sales efforts.

They can be highly-visible leaders and, because of their regular profile in leading with the big sale, they sometimes can be regarded as iconic in the SME, enjoying a high level of respect.

They carry a permanent aura of success, are busy, positive doers and enjoy 'the art of the deal', whether that is engaging in a direct sale process, or the more subtle activities related to making key contacts through networking.

Donald Trump is a prime example of the Seller leader. Though we cannot claim that 'The Don' is an SME leader, his extreme attributes really make the point:[22]

> *"I don't do it for the money. I've got enough, much more than I'll ever need. I do it to do it. Deals are my art form. Other people paint beautifully on canvas or write wonderful poetry. I like making deals, preferably big deals. That's how I get my kicks.*
>
> *Most people are surprised by the way I work. I play it very loose. I don't carry a briefcase. I try not to schedule too many meetings. I leave my door open. You can't be imaginative or entrepreneurial if you've got too much structure. I prefer to come to work each day and just see what develops.*
>
> *There is no typical week in my life. I wake up most mornings very early, around six, and spend the first hour or so of each day reading the morning newspapers. I usually arrive at my office by nine, and I get on the phone. There's rarely a day with fewer than 50 calls, and often it runs to over 100. In between, I have at least a dozen meetings. The majority occur on the spur of the moment, and few of them last longer than 15 minutes. I rarely stop for lunch. I leave my office by six-thirty, but I frequently make calls from home until midnight, and all weekend long.*
>
> *It never stops, and I wouldn't have it any other way. I try to learn from the past, but I plan for the future by focusing exclusively on the present. That's where the fun is. And if it can't be fun, what's the point?"*

Seller leaders, despite their sometime characteristic weaknesses in management, are driven by service. They usually have a view of customers that is similar to the distinctive and positive feature of many early entrepreneurial efforts.

---

[22]   Donald Trump & Tony Schwartz, *Trump: The Art of the Deal*, Random House USA, 1998.

The significant feature of this emphasis on service to customers is that it is in contrast to the more pushy sales process that relies on foot-in-the-door pressure tactics. Hence, it is a more powerful approach in the long run, in that it focuses on creating strong relationships through good customer experiences.

Seller entrepreneurs have a high degree of empathy, which transcends all of their business dealings and, indeed, their social interactions. They are very spontaneous, with a high level of persuasive talent, but, for most individuals with whom they come in contact, they will simply be perceived as 'nice people'.

They appreciate harmony in most situations and will work hard to see that this is achieved for all. Their empathy leads them to be extremely good listeners. They will be patient to a fault and very supportive of those who wish to communicate with them.

They like action and are more interested in the big picture of getting things done, than being slowed down by the devil that is in the detail. Their strong people skills mean that they are highly effective in the building and running of participative teams. A high degree of their effectiveness is related to an inherent intuition, built on their good listening skills and awareness of signals.

Sellers' collegiality and wish to please other people sometimes results in poor decision-making, in that keeping relations at the right level can have a higher level of priority than their concern for efficiency and achievement. Sometimes, they are more concerned about the feelings of others than they should be and this can get in the way of making optimal business decisions.

Over the years, we have observed a number of Seller leaders who have failed to realise their early potential. This often happens when the emerging pressures of the growing business divert them from their powerful main distinctive talent: selling.

Seller leaders should stick to what they do best – to be the company's prime external representative. Then they must ensure that they involve and engage individuals with the appropriate talents for the other STAR leadership functions.

The positive side to this is that, where such individuals are supported by a structured top-team process, their companies become highly effective much more quickly than the businesses led by other leadership types.

But, while they can be impulsive and sometimes procrastinating, overall their positive characteristics greatly outweigh the negative, in entrepreneurial activity in general and entrepreneurial selling in particular.

SELLER LEADERS – THE DARK SIDE

If this review of the qualities of a Seller leader appears too warm and cuddly, then we should also consider the reality, that what appears to be concern for others may be used sometimes in an exceedingly manipulative way.

There is a dark side to the Seller entrepreneur, analogous to the story of Narcissus, and indeed Seller entrepreneurs, like the Visionary entrepreneur, have strong narcissistic tendencies. When their narcissism leads them to see that they are the wonderful sales people they think they are, then that is a reinforcing factor and generally will be positively helpful to their sustained performance. However, if it leads to hubris in the same manner as experienced by some visionaries, then it can be very dangerous.

Sellers are good at selling and it comes naturally to them. While gazing at their own pretty reflection, they sometimes forget the other functions and aspects of the business that require equal attention, in particular the area of efficient management.

If the dark side of the Visionary entrepreneur is megalomaniac or autocrat, the dark side of the Seller entrepreneur can be Machiavellian manipulator or outright con-man. A notorious example of the dark side of the Seller leader is told by Ivan Fallon and James Srodes in their introduction to *DeLorean*:[23]

"In the cold, blue-grey flicker of the video monitor screen, the nagging question will not be silenced. What is that guy doing there? Every cop and dope pusher knows the rule: never make the buy yourself. Hand the cash

[23] Ivan Fallon & James Srodes, *Dream Maker: The Rise & Fall of John Z DeLorean*, Putnam, 1985.

over – but have someone else, somewhere else, take your delivery. But there is John DeLorean, media celebrity, international car tycoon, sitting in a Los Angeles airport hotel room that is so wired for sound it could generate a magnetic field.

What can DeLorean be thinking of? A man, back to the camera, opens a suitcase, displays the contents to DeLorean who is lounging casually on a couch. 'Between this and the other, it'll generate uh … about four and a half. Not less than four and a half mil'.

DeLorean stretches out a long arm and picks up one of the kilo bags of cocaine. 'It's as good as gold!' He gives a deep chuckle. 'Gold weighs more than this, for heaven's sake!'

Someone produces a bottle of champagne, passes around the glasses, with DeLorean jokingly venturing: 'I guess that is what they call "Just in the nick of time".' The incredulity mounts. Surely he must know that the FBI has paid for that champagne he is now raising tokenly to his lips? But his deep, resonant voice comes over as confidently and cheerfully as ever.

'Here's to a lot of success to everyone.' Everyone dutifully sips, although DeLorean himself is basically teetotal. He looks around. 'And for all those phone calls – thank you.' He laughs again.

It is at this point it comes: the knock on the door. DeLorean looks up with no sense of tension. Even now, he does not see the awful trap. The door opens and two men walk in. They share the good humour in the room. It's all a good joke. But the butt of the humour does not seem to realize it, even now.

'Hi, John,' says one of the newcomers, waving a badge in his face. 'I'm Jerry West of the FBI. You're under arrest for narcotics smuggling violations.'

It is a spectacular scene, one that will indelibly imprint itself on the world's imagination over a year later when the tapes finally make their TV debut. A look first of shock, then bewilderment crosses DeLorean's lean face. The handcuffs come out, slap around his left wrist. He offers the right wrist across the front of his body. Not good enough. Roughly, his hands are pulled behind him and the cuffs go on. We are left with that tall, gangling figure, head bent, standing above the coffee table which still contains the now closed suitcase full of cocaine, muttering 'I don't understand'.

Nor does the rest of the world. What is he doing there? What drove him to this? Can this really be the legend of Detroit, the saviour of Northern Ireland, the great all-American businessman with a social conscience and a dream?

The truth was that John DeLorean had no one else to make the buy for him. For all his legendary charisma, for all the money he had lavished on an army of hangers-on, he ended up alone that day. He had been called a maverick many times, and indeed he was – isolated from any satisfaction in his engineering talent or business accomplishments, an appealing personality, who could draw beautiful women and loyal aides, but who ultimately drove most of them way. This sad, lonely man ended up in a hotel-room drug trap because he could not bear to be found out, to confront his own failure.

This is the story of how John DeLorean began a public career that promised great hope and benefit to the world and how that promise was broken. It is the story of a man who once preached the social duties of the business executive, but who ended up cheating thousands of the poorest and hundreds of the richest people in the world – from Hollywood's exclusive Bel Air to the grimy slums of Belfast – and how he dared not be unmasked.

The lessons for the SME leader are to beware of hubris, greed, delusion, deceit, manipulation and the dark side of the seller.

The positive leadership behavioural characteristics of the SME Seller leader in pursuit of stellar growth are:
- Prospecting.
- Bonding.
- Closing.
- Networking.

PROSPECTING

Prospecting is the first stage of selling, when the courageous seller goes out into the market with hope, to try to identify potential customers. It is in principle, if not in harshness, like the experience of the 'forty-niners', who set off for California in search of riches in the 1849 gold rush.

These hardy pioneers headed into largely unknown territory, buoyed up with the thought of future riches. Just as with the sales prospector leaders of today, their challenges were who to talk to, where to look, what to look for, why is information relevant, when to stake a claim and how to exploit an opportunity.

In the modern era, if prospecting for success is not as physically demanding, it is just as difficult, with rich rewards coming only to a few of the thousands of hopefuls.

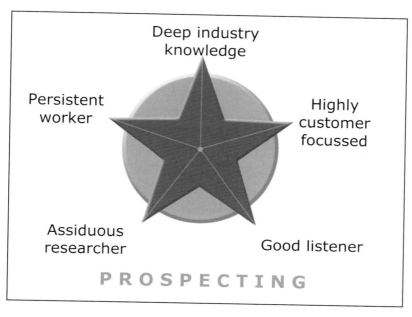

1. Deep industry knowledge

It is no surprise to us to note the current renewal of interest in apprenticeships, such as that served by Will in the textile trade, as the best way to acquire a deep knowledge of a business and its industry. Many successful SME leaders of today started at the bottom and worked their way upward to commercial success.

One of those is Brian McConville, who began his working life as an apprentice joiner, then started his own micro-business, which through enterprise and hard work he has developed into a leading international company.

But it wasn't all done only by hard work. In his early days, Brian learned the deep skills of joinery and the art of working with all kinds of woods. Later, he acquired a fascination with using advanced materials together with timber, to create unusual, innovative, specialist joinery solutions for customers.

This took Brian from joinery into shop-fitting and interiors. Ultimately, building on his foundational expertise, he expanded into the highly-technical business of ship-outfitting, where, due to his unique skills and knowledge, he has developed a stellar-growth SME that can count the largest cruise operators in the world as his customers.

In addition to his own capabilities, Brian has added strength to the company's competitive position by developing his team of top managers, a number of whom, just like Brian, started at the bottom and gained a deep knowledge of the industry on the way up.

> *"I believe I have a huge hunger for success, coupled with a zest for knowledge and understanding, not only business in general, but also how other businesses operate, so that I have a yardstick to measure my own success. Once gained from contacts and advisers, this knowledge has allowed me to take my own business in a more structured and focused direction."*

2. Highly customer-focussed

Having a strong focus on customers is an attitude often taken as a given by businesses, in that it seems so incontestable and obvious that, unfortunately, complacency sometimes sets in, especially on the back of perhaps early business success. The high importance of customer focus is undervalued, or is ignored, and managers fail to drive the ethos of this essential feature throughout their organisations. Seller leaders will not allow such a situation to arise.

A few years ago, Will was checking in for a late flight home from Gatwick to Belfast and, as happens at certain times, he was a bit grumpy after a long tiring day.

The airport was very busy with long queues, but the check-in staff were living in their own world, gossiping to each other about their holidays and paying minimum attention to the weary travellers.

As Will presented his ticket, the check-in clerk reached up and took it without comment, made no eye contact, carried on her animated conversation with her colleague about the relative merits of the clubs in Ibiza, printed the boarding card, slapped it on the counter without a word to Will, and without removing her gaze from her colleague, said *"Next!"* loudly in the middle of a sentence about how many rum and cokes she had drunk on one evening.

Will stood quietly, did not lift the boarding card, did not step to one side and did not say anything until the clerk became aware that he was still there. She stopped speaking to her friend, and looked up at Will, who said:

> *"Now can we try that again but, just for a change, this time why don't we pretend that I'm a customer?".*

Needless to say, the irony was completely lost on her, but at least it made Will feel better and gave the other travellers a laugh.

A high focus on customers is not all about cosseting and caring for the good ones. The highly-customer-focussed SME leader will get as much, and possibly a lot more, value for her company, by focussing on and getting rid of bad customers.

American Express, which knows what millions of people are spending, says that the 'best' customers outspend others by an average ratio of 14 to 1. By implication, this indicates that there are many 'poor' customers whose spending will do little to advance the prosperity of the enterprise, but yet who may consume inordinate amounts of service resource and, on closer examination, may turn out to be exceedingly unprofitable.

These unprofitable customers can attach themselves to an SME in an almost imperceptible way, in an accumulation of deadweight. It is the clear responsibility of the Seller leader to nip this debilitating process in the bud and periodically to carry out a cleansing audit of the customer list. Every company with which we have ever consulted has profited from such a focus.

3. Good listener

One of the critically important skills for a Seller leader is the ability to be a good listener, yet it is not surprising that these articulate, voluble, outgoing individuals sometimes find it difficult to pause sufficiently in order to listen effectively. Despite his renowned ability with words, Ernest Hemingway was an advocate of the value of listening in order to learn:

I like to listen. I have learned a great deal from listening carefully. Most people never listen.

Staying quiet and silent is not, of itself, any sign of being a good listener because, in order to learn, the silence must be used to allow the other party time to talk and to communicate potentially valuable information. The seller, paying careful attention all the while, can ask the next judicious question or give affirmation to what has been said.

Preparation is important in good listening. We have no less than Abraham Lincoln to validate this often-neglected behaviour:

When I am getting ready to reason with a man, I spend one-third of my time thinking about myself and what I am going to say – and two-thirds thinking about him and what he is going to say.

4. Assiduous researcher

Knowledge is power in most walks of life and certainly that is the case in business – or in prospecting for gold in 1849. Of course, there was the occasional lucky strike by a forty-niner, but those who really prospered over time were the prospectors who did the diligent geological research and staked their claims where workable deposits could be mined economically.

This is not to argue against speed and opportunism, but rather to make the point that often the Seller leader must be fast and thorough at the same time. Make the wrong call on accuracy and the forty-niner could be digging dirt for years, for no reward. Make the wrong call on speed and he is at the back of the queue for staking the mother-lode claim.

CDE Ireland Ltd specialises in the design and manufacture of customised, world-class aggregate processing equipment and is a striking example of research-led engineering expertise. The Cookstown-based SME's rapid growth is founded on chairman

Tony Convery's commitment to thorough fast research, which has delivered a strong competitive product offering for MD Brendan McGurgan to take to market.

Brendan articulates this commitment:

> *"The development of a strong product set has been fundamental to the firm's success. Taking a lead from Tony's original operation, we've invested heavily in research and development and established a set of really forward-thinking products. From this product-base, we develop aggregate solutions which are essentially designed and tailored specifically for the customer. We believe in making a product specifically for the customer's needs rather than making the customer fit the product and, now that we are in a global marketplace, the future is very exciting."*

5. Persistent worker

Anyone who has prospected for any length of time will have experienced the repeated sound of the word 'No', will have coped with rejection after rejection, and will know the difficulty of raising the motivation to set off on another cold, wet Tuesday morning's prospecting.

A high proportion of SME leaders either have started their business lives in the front line of selling, or have spent significant periods prospecting, often in export markets. Both these areas of experience require persistence of a high order. When we see advertisements for sales people, asking for 'self-starters' to apply, we know that this is code for 'extreme persisters'.

Calvin Coolidge was a fan of extreme persistence:

> *Nothing in the world can take the place of persistence. Talent will not; nothing is more common than the unsuccessful person with talent. Genius will not; unrewarded genius is almost a proverb. Education will not; the world is full of educated derelicts. Persistence and determination are omnipotent. The slogan 'press on' has solved, and always will solve, the problems of the human race.*

Persistence pays off. We agree, Calvin.

BONDING

The ability to bond with others is an essential characteristic for the Seller leader, due to the simple fact that, as individual or business consumers, provided all other things are roughly equal, generally we will buy from people we like.

This point is underlined by our own common sense and experience, allied to compelling research findings that positive eye contact, the use of a target's first name and a sincere smile are powerful, yet simple, factors in creating rapport.

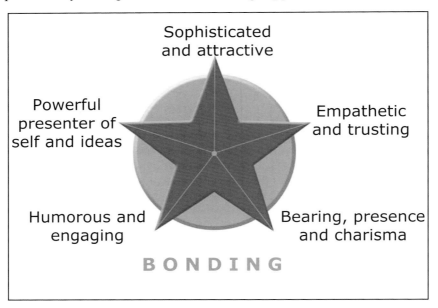

1. Sophisticated and attractive

Fundamentally, selling is about creating connections, so that effective communication can take place. It is important, therefore, that a SME Seller leader is an admired, attractive personality with a high level of genuine sophistication.

This characteristic is no artifice or pretence of any superiority over other people. Rather it is the product of deep experience, calm confidence and knowledge of how to handle relationships easily at the highest level, or comfortably relate to those lower in the hierarchy without any trace of condescension.

J enny Bristow is one of Northern Ireland's leading personalities and is well-known internationally for her regular networked TV cookery programme appearances. Through her obvious attractiveness and sophisticated, yet 'down-home', manner, Jenny has created a powerful, international Jenny Bristow brand. This has resulted in her becoming one of the UK's best-selling authors, leading to her website receiving hundreds of thousands of hits each month.

The Jenny Bristow brand carries attractiveness for consumers, a fact not lost on the major manufacturers who brand their products with her name, thus generating dramatically increased sales for the products concerned.

2. Empathetic and trusting

People who are empathetic and trusting generally make good sellers, because they are particularly effective in building long-term linkages with customers, colleagues and those whom they lead. They are seen as nice people. The unscrupulous sometimes will take advantage of their willingness to listen and to engage and may even capitalise on their demonstrable vulnerability, which is a feature of their trusting approach.

Certainly, sometimes, they can be hurt quite seriously in the business free-for-all but, in the long run, the compensations derived from their integrity-based relationships will more than outweigh any losses they may suffer because of their supposed naïvety.

As we have said before, Jack Welch certainly was not an SME leader but, in his last annual report as leader of the GE colossus, he made a statement on trust that is appropriate for any SME CEO :

... integrity establishes the trust that is so critical to the human relationships that make our values work. With trust, employees can take risks and believe us when we say a 'miss' doesn't mean career damage. With trust, employees can stretch performance goals and can believe us when we promise that falling short is not a punishable offence. Integrity and trust are at the heart of the informality we cherish. There are no witnesses needed to conversations, nor the need to 'put it in writing'. None of that – our word is enough.

R ichard Emanuel co-founded DX Communications in 1991 as a
tiny SME on a £3,000 overdraft. Eight years later, he sold it to
Cellnet for some £42m. His UK operations are now run under the
umbrella of ITS Investments, a successful, growing Scottish
company.

Richard has expanded into Europe in a major way, with the
acquisition of hundreds of retail stores. He now has 350 retail
outlets in Belgium and Holland and, in Scotland, has recently hired
a further 150 workers at his ITS plant in Renfrewshire.

This outstanding young entrepreneur appeared in *The Sunday
Times'* Rich List 2007 with wealth of £267 million, but to meet him in
person one is struck by his engaging openness, empathic approach
and evident trustworthiness.

We first heard him speak in public in the early 1990s before his
great success and he hasn't changed today. For all his stellar
achievements, Richard still retains the genuine humility of an
authentic STAR leader.

3. Bearing, presence and charisma

The classic leader of heroic status is male, tall, articulate and
charismatic, exuding quiet, determined confidence and attracting
loyal followers. None of us can do anything about our gender or
our height. The good news for most of us, as evidenced by the
current crop of SME leaders and some of the iconic leaders such as
Meg Whitman of eBay and the vertically-challenged Jack Welch, is
that these two characteristics of the classic leader may not be so
important after all.

One instant and simple way to enhance bearing, presence and
charisma is for a leader to increase dramatically what he or she
pays for a business suit. £2,000 on anyone's back will make them
feel better, look more confident and look sharper. In many cases,
how we look is how we act, and buying a really good suit can start
a virtuous circle.

In recent years, the trend for dressing down to casual attire in
business has opened an opportunity for leaders to go against the

trend and 'power-dress' in the best sense of the term – for cynics on this subject, this really does work.

There is ample evidence that confident bearing, distinguished presence and an indefinable charisma will attract enthusiastic followers. One young Irish entrepreneur who fits the bill is Oliver Tattan, who has built a team in Vivas Health to take on the oligopolist giants in the industry. He and his team have raised a strong lobbying voice, to speak for change and a loosening of restriction in the health insurance industry in Ireland.

In addition to having the demonstrable behavioural competences of a leader, Oliver Tattan is always immaculately dressed, which enhances his obvious bearing, presence and charisma – superb tailoring helps us all.

In April 2008, Hibernian Insurance reached a deal to take a significant stake in Vivas, Oliver's company. The exact terms of the agreement were not disclosed, but it is believed that an enterprise value was placed on the business which would result in Oliver Tattan receiving €10 million for his holding.

4. Humorous and engaging

One of the most effective ways of keeping strong bonds in a workforce, when rapid growth is causing stress and fracturing relationships, is the easy use of humour by the leader. Laughter is very infectious and can quickly relieve tension, if it is used naturally and judiciously in work, even when tense demanding situations may seem inappropriate occasions for a joke. But it takes a particular type of talent to do this successfully and to ensure that the joke does not backfire, through bad timing or bad telling.

Roger Troughton rescued the troubled, world-famous Belleek Pottery in the 1980s and restored it to profitability over a period of three years.

Those were three tough years, of harsh unremitting driving, from this larger-than-life personality. To be frank, Roger's regular abusiveness was very difficult to cope with, for those of us who had to endure the metaphoric lash of his tongue.

He was a hard, uncompromising, often capricious man – and yet, in spite of his sometimes fearsome persona, he inspired great loyalty from the people who helped him to lay the foundations for Belleek's current success.

This loyalty was created partly because Roger had the innate, plain-speaking humility of the common Yorkshireman. Most of all, it was because he had a wonderful sense of humour, which he shared with everyone, regardless of rank. He could be fearsome but, also, he was great fun to work with.

Everyone who came in contact with Roger, whether from his career as a trouble-shooter in the giant Jefferson Smurfit Group, or when he owned the stellar-growth SME Belleek Pottery, has a fund of hilarious stories from their time working with him. Strangely, most of the frequent nightmares are forgotten.

5. Powerful presenter of self and ideas

This characteristic is at the centre of effective leadership, in that a leader needs followers and followers are best attracted by persuasive communication.

There is a well-documented historical danger that the best deliverers of persuasive power sometimes may misuse their talent for evil purpose; in the way that the dynamic rhetoric of Adolf Hitler led Germany and its people into initially successful, but ultimately disastrous, confrontation with the Allies.

In the vast majority of cases, whether in the political arena or in the sphere of business, the powerful presentation of self or ideas is for positive purposes and, in business, no one does it better than the great Irish tycoon and raconteur, Sir Anthony O'Reilly. He makes such presentations look so effortless and easy – but the key is thorough preparation.

S ome years ago, a friend of Will's attended the Irish Management Institute's annual conference in the beautiful lakeside setting at Killarney, at which Tony O'Reilly was the main speaker, due on stage at 11 am.

At 7 am that morning, when out for a brisk walk, Will's friend heard the loudspeakers in the auditorium relaying the voice of a speaker. Knowing that no speeches were due for another two hours, out of curiosity he diverted the path of his walk and went in to see what was going on. There were two people in the vast auditorium: Dr O'Reilly on the podium practising the delivery of his speech and one of his assistants listening at the back of the hall.

If an admired public speaker with the ability of Sir Anthony O'Reilly sees the need to practise in order to deliver an effective message, then the lesson on preparation is clear to all SME Seller leaders seeking to influence any audience.

Effective communication through presentation is a key talent for seller leaders in that there is no neutrality; a slip-shod approach will have damaging effects on the leader's bonding with followers, while a superb performance will result in significant added value for the enterprise. But presenting self and ideas for the benefit of a business is about more than just making a speech, as is clear from Tony O'Reilly's stellar track record.

I n 1982 a young man called Colin Anderson presented himself and his ideas to the world of business, when he started a one-man advertising agency. At that time, facing competition from large long-established firms, the outlook was far from bright and, indeed, many people forecasted that the upstart would fail.

Through force of personality and courageous creativity, Colin built Anderson Advertising [now ASG] into one of Ireland's leading marketing services groups.

His success was recognised as early as 1997, when he was awarded the OBE for his services to industry.

Colin's ability to present himself and his ideas for the benefit of the enterprises in which he is involved goes well beyond the stellar success of his own SME group of companies, as is evident in the great progress of what is now the Northern Ireland Screen Commission. Under his chairmanship, the Commission led the development of a film and television industry in Northern Ireland, taking it from almost nothing to a multi-million pound industry within seven years. He often says he believes in "making it happen with attention to detail", which is hard to argue with.

Colin Anderson's rise from humble beginnings was powered by his own forceful ability to present himself as a role-model leader and an engaging persuasiveness that enabled his creative ideas to be brought to life.

CLOSING

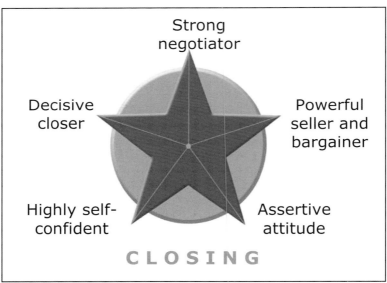

1. Strong negotiator

County Down native Terence Brannigan learned his trade in negotiation while working with Sir Gerry Robinson in building the giant Compass group in Britain. Returning to Northern Ireland in 2006 to acquire the £30 million turnover Maybin Support Services, he put those skills to immediate good use and, within two years, through swift, strong deal-making, he created a £150 million business, employing 15,000 people throughout the UK and Ireland.

Terence's first move was to quickly snap up Maybin's closest rival, Grove Services, on which he commented:

> *"Grove had some key customers which we wanted to have on board and it was active in some services areas that we wanted to get into. But the key reasoning for us was that a number of national players had also tried to buy Maybin and we knew that they might be tempted to buy the No.2 in the marketplace as a route into Northern Ireland. So, to put it bluntly, we shut the door in their faces."*

With dominance assured in Northern Ireland, the team then looked at the Republic and three deals followed in quick succession, to vault Terence Brannigan's company to No.1 position in Ireland. At this point, he rebranded the entire business under the name 'resource'.

Terence has recruited a strong leadership team to support him as he pursues further growth and further acquisition targets:

> *"This is a team which I've every confidence can drive us onwards to our target turnover of £250 million".*

The company now operates from bases throughout the UK and Ireland, but the strong negotiator from County Down is true to his roots:

> *"... the headquarters of this business will be, and will always be, here in Northern Ireland. ... we are not looking over our shoulders at the so-called big nationals. We **are** a big national ...".*

2. Powerful seller and bargainer

A graphic way to observe powerful selling and bargaining in process, in its most basic and effective form, is in the street-markets of our great cities. In the staccato, rapid-fire delivery of the barrow-boy seller, together with personal comment on, and engagement with, passersby, in an effort to get them to stop and listen to the intuitively-crafted, and often brilliantly-pitched, value propositions, this street theatre can be a master-class in bargaining and selling for the interested observer.

Having caught the attention of a prospect, the barrow-boy immediately locks on, like a heat-seeking missile on its target, and pursues the sales opportunity with unrelenting tenacity. As the target ducks and weaves evasively, he follows every turn, overcoming objections, presenting new angles and, all the time, getting closer, ever closer until the successful hit is made.

A supplier selling product to these barrow-boy bargainers, as Will has done, will experience the identical process in reverse action, but absolutely as effective in outcome for the living-by-his-wits buyer.

Our experience is that the ability to sell and bargain to world-class standard is generally innate, or formed early in life. It is rather like the innate talent of a world-class golfer.

While training and professional guidance can improve performance significantly for the average Joe in this field, the God-given, intuitive skills of the market trader always will mark out the real STAR sellers and buyers. These talented individuals will often be seen leading stellar-growth SMEs – and sometimes just running a market stall.

3. Assertive attitude

To fit the bill as an effective closer, there is little point in being a shrinking violet, humbly and generously giving way on every occasion. The crucial attitude of assertiveness for the successful leader is well-exemplified by Michelle Mone, the straight-talking Glaswegian inventor of the *Ultimo* bra and founder of MJM International.

F rom an early age, Michelle was fixated on making it in business and was in no way put off by the accepted wisdom, that it is harder for women to succeed than it is for men. Her attitude is that, while there is real truth in this, the key reason that more women do not succeed lies in their lack of ambition:

"*I have got where I am because I wanted it. If you're not prepared to work for it, you'll never get it. There's no secret to being successful, it's just a lot of hard work*".

MJM has shown stellar-growth in a relatively short time and, even though its founder is still only 36 years old, it is well-established as one of the UK's top lingerie companies, carrying five brands, with a home workforce of 120 and 1,500 people working in China.

Michelle's most recent success is the opening of a chain of Ultimo retail branches in Debenhams and she is forthright in sending a signal to her competitors:

> *"I think the High Street should be concerned. We'll have the price points, the quality, the best fitting bras in the market and the shops. They should be frightened".*

This assertive attitude reputedly is reflected also in her uncompromising stance with employees, as she drives the leadership of her SME. She is energetic, sometimes upsetting staff, and always upfront with her assertive views:

> *"I would say I'm firm but fair. I wouldn't say I was a nasty bitch or anything, though others probably would. If you're a man in business and you're tough, then you're a hero. If you're a woman and you're tough and direct, then you're a bitch".*

4. Highly self-confident

The possession of self-confidence is an attribute that imbues the SME leader with strengths in almost every dimension but, arguably, has its most significant application in the area of closing deals or sales. The fundamental reason for this is that high self-confidence equips the leader with a high level of risk-tolerance and, hence, the ability to accept 'No' for an answer and to walk away from a deal. But that is not all.

The possession of high self-belief equips a person with the persistent drive to try longer, harder and with more intensity than their competitors, which greatly increases their chances of eventual success. Further, that success of itself will breed higher and higher expectations, increasing the leader's already strong self-confidence.

There is no doubt that leaders who have a high expectation of success will put more effort into the achievement of goals than those who do not believe with the same fervour.

Willie John McBride is recognised as one of the greatest leaders in rugby, having captained Ireland and led the all-conquering 1974 British & Irish Lions. His self-confidence is infectious and he has the enduring characteristic of the truly self-confident leader: he can tell a self-deprecating story against himself.

At the 'Wooden Spoon' dinner in Belfast in 2004, Willie John was the guest of honour, addressing hundreds of leading rugby personalities and journalists. This was his introduction to his speech:

> *"Many years ago, after I stopped playing top-flight rugby, I went regularly with a group of friends to play touch-rugby at Ballyclare Rugby Club, just to keep some level of fitness.*
>
> *One night in the middle of winter, it was pouring with rain when I went down to the clubhouse and there was only one other person there – a wee fella called Will McKee. Neither of us was all that keen to go out but we went anyway, thinking the others would show up soon. We squelched over the pitch and, by now, the rain was coming down in torrents, so we jogged to the tall hedge for some shelter. By this time, we were soaked through.*
>
> *For some minutes, we stood in miserable silence, waiting for the others and getting wetter and wetter, until Will suddenly said to me:*
>
>> *"Willie John, you are famous all over the world as a great rugby player. You have played in the biggest stadiums, before hundreds of thousands of people. At the height of your fame, never in your wildest dreams did you think that someday you would be standing under a hawthorn bush in Ballyclare, soaked to the skin and up to your ankles in muck."*

It brought the house down.

5. Decisive closer

Decisive closing is about timing, process and determination. Of prime importance is knowing when to summarise the discussion with the right words and knowing when to ask for the order.

Skill in the process of closing, through looking for buying signals, can be taught, but timing is the more important factor in ensuring a successful outcome. Ask too quickly and the prospect is not ready; wait too long and the moment of opportunity has passed. But the greatest, and altogether too common, weakness is for the seller not to ask for the order at all.

The key question does not revolve round the fears or errors that may cause the missed timing or failure to ask. It is mainly a question of decisiveness and a determined seizing of the moment.

A certain amount of training can help, of course, but real improvement will only come through repeated experience.

The ability to close deals decisively is a powerful weapon for the SME leader, not only for its positive effect on the commercial success of the company, but also for its motivational influence on the people whose livelihood depends on the completed transactions.

The leaders of publicly-quoted corporations, who through indecision or poor negotiating skills regularly fail to complete deals quickly, may find that their weakness in this regard can cost them their jobs. For the leader of an SME, it can cost his job, livelihood, company and perhaps even his house.

NETWORKING

Networking, in the form of meeting with and making contacts, itself is a form of selling or, with a narrower interpretation, can be regarded as a vital component within the total selling process.

Certainly, its aims are broadly the same as pure selling, in that it positions the company, communicates at a generally high level and establishes linkages, which may result in direct sales revenue.

In a stellar-growth SME, its operation rarely can be delegated in the same way that a Seller leader can delegate the acquisition of sales. Effective networking is a highly personalised activity, with the chief characteristic that it must be subtle. Too brash and overt an approach will repel rather than attract, but too reticent an approach simply will be ineffective. The requirement for a Seller leader is to build a strong contact base, be active and busy within it, be aware of rich PR leverage opportunities, be highly respected and be very well known.

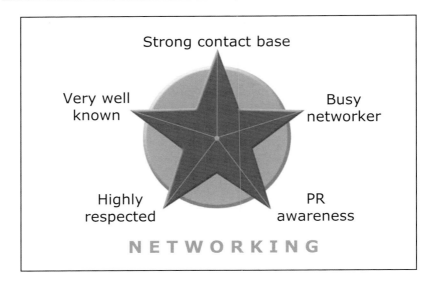

1. Strong contact base

Building a strong contact base is the vital first ingredient of a robust networking strategy. It is generally the result of years of steady accrual rather than rapid build-up, due to the fact that its building blocks consist of individual personal relationships nurtured over time.

The networking leader will be a prospector, in much the same way as he initiates product sales and, in the process, will reach a wide audience of potentially-valuable contacts. The significant difference is that, while he targets sales projects carefully, only some of which will prove profitable, the simple, often-overlooked, fact is that, over time, all networking contacts carry value.

The constraints of time will limit the number of events any one person can attend and, therefore, an element of targeting will prove useful, but the importance of even the most casual contacts should not be underestimated. Their value is often negated only by a lack of imagination on the part of the networker.

Another key attribute is the compunction to follow through on initially-promising leads. Follow-up is relatively easy and just requires very simple reminders and activities – but it is almost invariably neglected by most people, leaving a terrific opportunity for differentiation to the rare SME leader who actually does follow through.

2. Busy networker

Having established a growing contact base, all the networker has to do to ensure real value outcomes is to be busy in attending the right events to keep the relationships warm and to meet the influential people, who through their own lists of contacts, will enable additional leverage.

D erry O'Donovan, a leading banker with AIB Bank, is a consummate networker, whose strong contact base, developed over the years, has brought great value to the bank generally, and in particular to its dealings with the agricultural sector, in which Derry is directly involved.

It is an education to watch this busy networker in action, as he works the room in any of the many gatherings he attends. He is never intrusive, is always extremely courteous and everybody seems to like him.

While these are skills possessed by many people, what marks Derry out as special is his busyness; the number of individuals to whom he can talk in a short space of time and the fact that each contact is meaningful.

The Seller leader must be disciplined and must set aside time to engage in networking activity, together with ensuring that he has the social skills to maximise coverage of the targeted contacts, who over time may bring value to his business.

The importance of effective networking is underlined by AG Lafley, CEO of Procter & Gamble:

The measure of a powerful person is that their circle of influence is greater than their circle of control.

3. PR awareness

With promotional costs of all kinds at astronomical levels, the awareness and effective use of PR tactics can wrest advantage away from the biggest of advertising or promotional spenders.

T he CEO of the relative minnow Newbridge Networks, competing against the giant Cisco Systems at a major industry show in Geneva, tells a great story about the success achieved by his marketing director, Brian Keating:

> *"We knew well that Cisco were going to spend enough money to grab all the headlines, dominate the show and totally eclipse our relatively meagre presence, even though we were intending to display all our new products; but when we heard that they had booked Michael Jackson to do repeated live performances, we thought our spend was going to be for nothing.*
>
> *Brian Keating, our marketing director, had other ideas and scrapped the original plans. We set up a completely open stand with a background resembling a stadium, laid artificial grass on the stand and got a group of tattooed Maoris to perform a ferocious, energetic 'Haka'. The energy of these guys and the racket they made drew hundreds of people and, by the middle of the show, we were drawing twice the media attention Michael Jackson and Cisco were getting. And on a miniscule budget".*

Brian Keating's Geneva brilliance in creating competitive power from very limited resource is an example of PR entrepreneurship in action and illustrates the applicability of the well-known definition of an entrepreneur:

> *An entrepreneur is someone who pursues business opportunities, beyond known resources, to create wealth.*

4. Highly respected

One of the key questions to be answered for any networker seeking to make an important contact is 'Will he take my call?'. Whether it will be possible to get past the gatekeeper depends on the caller's reputation and the respect with which he is viewed.

Respect may come from the esteem with which the leader is held in the business community, but it may also stem in part from a high profile in social activity.

E ric Cairns is one of Ireland's most successful estate agents and property developers, with a highly-respected reputation for leadership within his industry. Eric's networking talent was to put his own name over the door of his business and then build that name into one of Ireland's premier brands.

Further, Eric, as an outstanding public speaker and personality, is also acknowledged as the promoter of many charitable causes, for which he has raised substantial funding.

Most business-people, politicians, civil servants or influential individuals will take a call from Eric Cairns.

5. Very well-known

Fame and prominence is a powerful opener of doors for networking, as is evidenced by the ability of personalities such as Bono to walk with ease into the Oval Office or the Vatican.

The SME networker will not find things just so simple but Seller leaders will increase their relative influence immensely by pro-actively leveraging their own opportunities for fame, however modest by comparison.

The leader does not need a level of fame that guarantees access to the White House. The secret is to target an area of interest for the company's customers, or whatever segment will bring advantage, and then build a high-profile position by focussing on the opportunity. This can be achieved by for example, taking on the chairmanship of a sports club or sponsoring a major event.

The old saying is very true in the context of networking: 'It is better to be a big fish in a small pond, than a small fish in a big pond'.

SELLER LEADER

Score yourself on each of the behaviours of the Seller Leader below, using the following scoring range:

5 This is one of my outstanding characteristics. I demonstrate this much more than other leaders.

4 This is one of my key strengths. However, I think I could improve on my practice of this behaviour.

3 Sometimes I do this, but not often enough.

2 One of my weaker areas. I rarely demonstrate this. The behaviour does not sit well with me.

1 I don't use this behaviour and doubt if I could.

Total your score. The maximum score achievable is 100, so your score can be expressed as a percentage.

PROSPECTING		BONDING	
Deep industry knowledge	☐	Sophisticated and attractive	☐
High customer focus	☐	Empathetic and trusting	☐
Good listener	☐	Bearing, presence and charisma	☐
Assiduous researcher	☐	Humorous and engaging	☐
Persistent worker	☐	Powerful presenter of self and ideas	☐

CLOSING		NETWORKING	
Strong negotiator	☐	Great contact base	☐
Powerful seller and bargainer	☐	Busy networker	☐
Assertive attitude	☐	PR awareness	☐
Highly self-confident	☐	Highly respected	☐
Decisive closer	☐	Very well-known	☐

Seller Total %

Now transfer your score to page **206**.

7
THE MANAGER LEADER

In the popular press, the word 'manager' does not sit well with the words 'leader' or 'entrepreneur'. Managers are perceived as being dull, bureaucratic, focussed on routine, efficiency and with little empathy for other people. This sounds a bit like a general description of the typical characteristics of accountants and, in many cases, that is not far off the mark.

However, in our experience, the Manager leader of an SME – with the undoubted advantage that accounting skills bring – has the highest statistical chance of success of all who attempt to start, develop and grow businesses. Yes, they are driven by efficiency, are cost-conscious and highly-literate financially, and yes, they do like to be in control and in the place of power. But, often, they also are very effective marketers and sellers and they are distinctively good at process. Looked at in the long run, of all our SME leader types, they are the most likely to stay with the business from its early days of start-up, through growth and development, into a global business of significance.

They are growth leaders, with a strong focus on the bottom line, and they lead by their powers of general management and process. Employees may not particularly enjoy working for them, but they do feel secure within the well-run business structure.

Sometimes, uninformed commentators describe senior corporate executives in general as entrepreneur leaders, and do not draw any distinction between the operation of an SME and that of a LargeCo, but patently this is an error. Our experience, and significant research over the years, backed up by both common sense and widespread third-party academic investigation, tells us that they may look similar – but, in the make up of their personality and the things they have to do, they are very different as managers. The businesses they run are also very different from each other.

Top corporate executives who have stuck the pace and climbed the career ladder relentlessly, in the main, are unlikely to show the clear behavioural patterns of the Visionary, Seller, or Innovator entrepreneur leader. Significantly, some will show the Manager and Team-builder leader patterns, but only those who have been lucky enough to achieve sufficient reward and satisfaction from being within an exciting, growing, entrepreneurially-driven corporate organisation.

'Manager leader' is not an oxymoron. It may seem to be so, in that much of the classic view of entrepreneurial activity is related to the pioneering individual going out, and without any boring management grind, achieving great goals against all odds. But, in the complex business environment of today, the myth and the reality are some distance apart. Maybe it was always so.

Once a business gets to the size where it has multiple customers, multiple employees and multiple products, its survival in the short or long-term depends on good management. Most Manager leaders we have observed have other strong leadership pattern features, in addition to their predominant feature.

Manager leaders frequently have a strong accounting or financial background and are extremely ambitious. They have a strong desire for upward mobility, whether in their own SME business or in a larger corporation, and the key for them is a wish to find opportunities to realise value from what they perceive as their particular talents.

They perform well in corporate leadership positions and are generally very confident people, with a high level of personal self-esteem. If their corporate employer does not deliver for them in the way that they feel they deserve, they are confident enough to get up and move on. They are a rich resource to the entrepreneurial strength of any region.

Like the Visionary leader, the Manager leader is generally a decisive individual who gets things done.

MANAGER LEADERS – THE DARK SIDE

Where the application of Frederick Taylor's scientific management is applied without the humane touch its author had intended, the life-sapping potential is real. This was well-known to millions of workers in the massive factories that were the engines of growth for early to mid-20th century industrial economies. But there was an even darker side, where countless lives were literally destroyed.

After World War I, many German companies were influenced by a militaristic culture of management, its associated stern discipline and authoritative imposition of systems and processes. Then, in the 1930s, most of the great names of German industry, to a greater or lesser degree, supported the rise of the Nazis. Indeed, IG Farben, Thyssen and Deutsche Bank financed Hitler's election campaign in 1933 and, later, the giant Krupp organisation became his most valuable industrial ally.

At this time, the Nazis were adopting and encouraging an idealistic form of scientific management to 'produce benefit for the German people' but, in a very few years, things were to take an altogether more sinister twist when the SS became directly involved with Krupp.

Alfried Krupp and his father, Gustav, initially were hostile to the Nazi Party but, in 1933, Alfried joined the SS. As a result of the terms of the Versailles Treaty, the Krupp family had been forced to become producers of agricultural machinery after World War I. However, on Alfried joining the SS, Krupp factories began producing tanks under what was officially part of the Agricultural Tractor Scheme. With the Krupp industrial muscle, they also built submarines in Holland and new weapons were developed and tested in Krupp establishments in Sweden.

After hostilities commenced in the World War II, Alfried Krupp ensured that a continuous supply of his firm's tanks, munitions and armaments reached the German Army. He also was responsible for moving whole industrial factories from occupied countries back to Germany, where they were rebuilt and put into production by the Krupp company, in support of the Nazi war machine.

The dark side of management really was exposed when Krupp also built factories in German-occupied countries and ran them with rational efficiency, using the forced slave labour of over 100,000 inmates of concentration camps. This included a fuse factory inside Auschwitz itself. Many of the prisoner slave-labourers were also moved to Silesia to build a major arms factory there.

It is estimated that around 70,000 of these wretched, oppressed workers died as a direct result of the brutal scientific methods of management, acquiesced to by the managers and most cruelly implemented by the guards of these iniquitous Krupp establishments.

The positive leadership behavioural characteristics for the stellar-growth Manager leader are:
- Planning.
- Executing.
- Leveraging.
- Profiting.

PLANNING

While planning and forecasting are often treated as the same thing, there is a significant difference between the two. Companies plan, precisely because of the difficulty in foreseeing or forecasting the future.

The first requirement for an effective planning system is to make it thoroughly systematic, because of its vital contribution to the successful achievement of aims.

Rudyard Kipling's poem highlights the questions to be asked by the Manager leader at the planning stage:

I keep six honest serving-men,
They taught me all I knew;
Their names are What and Why and When,
And How and Where and Who.

Leaders frequently get caught up with the excitement of the latest project or sales opportunity and skip over some of the key questions – to their subsequent cost. The Manager leader asks all the right questions, carefully analyses the answers and assembles the data in meticulous, well-constructed plans.

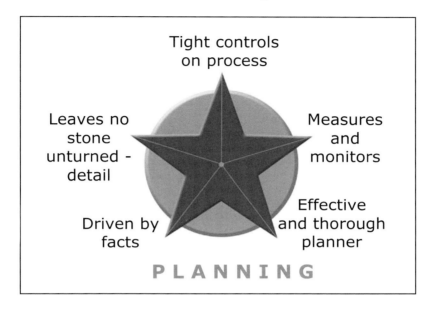

1. Tight controls on process

Control is a crucial element in effective management. It is notoriously difficult to implement in this competitive era, which has moved away from the command and control model of earlier times to a greater freedom, allowing entrepreneurial input at all levels of a business.

From a group of farm buildings in Carryduff, Northern Ireland, Gerry Lowe built a worldwide refrigeration-hire business, which grew to become the market leader and the most competitive player in its niche.

Lowe Refrigeration's focus on detailed planning, under Gerry's direction, was its key competitive advantage and enabled this small Irish company to have a global market reach.

Gerry's training as a chartered accountant stood him in good stead as he developed the logistics support system that allowed Lowe Refrigeration to ship the right refrigeration units to international food shows, to arrive at the right time and be supported by a first-class customer service system.

I n another sector, brothers Brian and Niall Irwin have implemented meticulous process controls at their Portadown bakery, which serves major multiple retailers throughout the UK and Ireland. An obsession with these controls enables them to deliver competitive unit costs and the continuance of their company's stellar-growth.

2. Measures and monitors

Measurement of performance requires a deep understanding of the business on the part of the Manager leader. The first step is to enable the selection and application of relevant metrics. Having established a robust, accurate system of measurement, the next, unendingly repetitive, task is to implement a monitoring procedure that records, collates and analyses the acquired data and provides the management information to enable the leadership team to make daily decisions.

This applies to all activity areas of the company, such as procurement, manufacturing, selling and distribution, but is particularly important in finance generally, and cash flow in particular. 'What gets measured, gets done' is a truism, but its familiarity does not make it any less relevant or vital.

Among the dangers the Manager leader must watch for are over-zealous application of measurement and monitoring, which can kill the entrepreneurial spirit on which competitive advantage is built in a business. But it is a fine balance, because the tight measurement of activity is a fundamental driver of commercial competitiveness, from careful management of processing costs to close monitoring of sales performance and the all-important focus on cash.

The classic example of the monitoring leader – arguably carried to extreme – is that of Harold Geneen, who built the mighty ITT corporation, basing its management on meticulous attention to 'the numbers', with the careers of long-serving business unit managers rising or falling at Geneen's monthly, nerve-shatteringly intense, inquisitions. Many commentators feel that Geneen's focus on measurement became an obsession and, ultimately, its restrictive effects led to the break-up of the mighty ITT empire.

3. Effective and thorough planner

We have worked with many highly-successful SME leaders who, leading from the front, get carried away with the heady exhilaration of growth and, in the excitement, lose sight of the perhaps more mundane responsibility of thorough planning.

Despite short-term progress, the manager leader will not lose sight of the need to establish clear objectives, to amass relevant data diligently, to explore a range of viable scenarios, to evaluate their relative value and to select a recommended course of action.

I an Cargill works as a planning consultant with Linkubator Ltd in assisting companies to develop coherent and effective business plans. He is a Manager leader *par excellence*. His greatest strengths are his laser-like focus on the facts, allied to an ice-cold objectivity, both of which ensure that the many business plans in which he is involved are produced to the highest quality level.

It is interesting to observe the degree of respect from colleagues that Ian engenders through his thorough approach to planning. His strategy is to focus on the planning process itself as being more valuable than the end product plan. This creates a continuing engagement of all participants, producing the best possible result in terms of accuracy of the plan and committed buy-in on the part of those who have to oversee its implementation.

4. Driven by facts

It is foolish to assume that the rational accumulation of vital facts, however accurate and relevant they are, of itself can deliver stellar-growth to an SME, if crucial judgement and intuitive flair is missing. However, the manager who neglects the importance of facts certainly will not qualify by any standard as an effective Manager leader of a stellar-growth SME.

Getting the facts generally is within the capability of an assiduous team, but fast-growing SMEs, and indeed their larger counterparts, sometimes struggle with the effective application of this valuable knowledge. An example is commonly evident in that singularly significant element of the ongoing planning process – budgeting.

A common budgeting characteristic in very large companies or public sector organisations is the practice of 'padding', where a business unit leader sets and negotiates a higher operating expenditure budget than he really requires, in order to ease his life in the ensuing period.

In an SME, the room for political manoeuvre may not be sufficiently lax to allow this sort of cynical manipulation, but we have observed a factor within SMEs that can interfere insidiously with both the setting of fact-based budgets and the planning process itself. Greed.

Greed at the top, where controlling leaders personally take more out of the company than the balance-sheet facts justify.

Remember that facts are gathered by people and budgets are set by people – people are influenced by the activities and behaviours of their leaders. Where there is behaviour of excess by senior executives, then the operatives will take a lead and compromise facts to suit themselves, rather than the needs of the business.

The Manager leader will stamp out excess at all levels and maintain, from top to bottom, a laser focus on accurate facts.

5. Leaves no stone unturned – detail

Judgement and intuition are needed, not only for interpretation of data, but to know where to look and how to extract the detail that will deliver competitive advantage. Doggedly searching among reams of seemingly-opaque data is hard work but often can repay the attention to detail by uncovering information that has been missed by the competition. If 'the devil is in the detail', then arguably the profit may also lie there too.

The Manager leader will search for the little things that don't look or feel quite right and will then drill into the specific detail on process, HR, finance, sales or whatever has caused the unease.

R ory Byrne, owner and founder of the £10 million Powder Byrne ski company, thinks much of the secret of his success has been due to his eye for detail:

"I am always looking for ways to do things better. I have a phenomenal eye for detail, which in the office can be positively annoying. Visually, I am a perfectionist and I will pick up on the tiniest thing that isn't important to anyone else but me. When I see something wrong, I want to put it right".

EXECUTING

Larry Bossidy, one of the greatest business leaders of modern times, argues passionately against those who regard matters of execution as detail work, which can and should be left to the lower levels of the business dealing with process and delivery:

Many people regard execution as detail work that's beneath the dignity of a business leader. That's wrong. To the contrary, it's a leader's most important job.

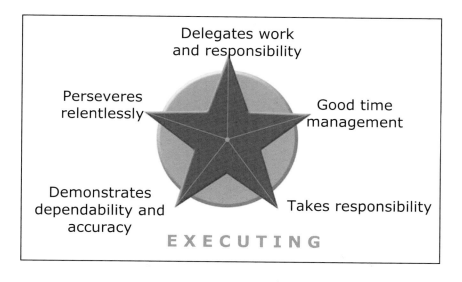

Larry has run some of the largest corporations in the world but, here, he speaks for the SME Manager leader. Effective execution is all-important.

1. Delegates work and responsibility

In our work with fast-growing SMEs, we regularly see them spurt towards stellar growth and then, for no obviously apparent reason, the wheels start to come off and growth stalls. In a high proportion of cases, closer examination shows that failure to delegate work and responsibility effectively has strangled the early promise.

There is a real problem here, in that, in its early days, an SME often has only one outstanding executive – the founder – and, therefore, with the best intentions in the world, there is simply no one to whom responsibility can be delegated at that time. The solution, of course, is to bring additional talent on board and the sooner this happens, the better, for the founder and for the business.

The associated problem for a founder in this position – where to bring on additional staff when the costs are already stretched – is that often the only way to deal with the dilemma is to get rid of existing, less-capable people. The impasse that this decision can cause should not be underestimated. Firm and resolute action must be taken by the Manager leader, so that the company's growth is maintained.

2. Good time management

The first rule of good time management is never being late, yet many otherwise competent business executives are careless with its execution.

O ne of the best preparations for business life that Will received was from his father, John's grandfather, who was a stickler for timekeeping. No matter what the appointment was for, or however minor its importance, once a time had been agreed, then it must be honoured or he would create a most fearsome row.

In Will's early, more tardy days, any failure to keep to rigid time resulted in old John giving him a robust clip on the ear, which had the desired effect. Not acceptable in the modern world perhaps but, even today, Will is never late for appointments!

The Manager leader manages time by pro-active programming of activity rather than reacting to events and thus allowing the urgent to dominate at the expense of the important.

3. Takes responsibility

Individual responsibility is the element of culture within an organisation that can enable relatively small SMEs to punch well above their weight and to compete effectively with much larger organisations. This is what gives the SME flexibility and speed of movement, but it will only be present where responsibility is clearly taken by the leader and is encouraged within the business as 'the way we do things round here – every one of us'.

Getting the message across that the leader takes responsibility needs explicit statements of intent, demonstrable examples of behaviour in taking the blame as well as the credit, and subtle signals that the boss, as an individual, will do his share of the rough work, if necessary.

W hen Kevin Quigley, COO of Garage Door Systems, sees his loading team under pressure to complete a load for a ferry sailing, he will join in the lifting to help the men that he rightly sees as his colleagues. This is not mere tokenism. It is repaid by the readiness of the loading team and others in the company to take individual responsibility and to go to the assistance of their workmates, as required, in order to get the job done.

Creating a culture where responsibility is owned by individuals requires clear leadership, role example and active execution by the entire top team of the company.

4. Demonstrates dependability and accuracy

The Manager leader who demonstrates dependability and accuracy performs one of the most vital tasks of a leader in giving his followers security of mind. Volatility and mercurial talent on the part of a CEO sometimes can bring benefit to certain business situations, but confidence is instilled in a team or workforce through knowing that the leader will react in a particular way and can be depended on to make accurate judgements.

I n addition to his role as a director and consultant with Linkubator, Ian Cargill runs a financial support and accountancy practice and counts a number of fast-growth SMEs among his clients. Ian is a supremely logical thinker who delivers his judgements and opinions exactly as he sees them, without any veneer or emotion.

For a first-time client, this cold douche of logic can be a shock to the system after the lukewarm, and comparatively expensive, cosseting he is accustomed to receiving from a 'Big 4' firm. But when the client sees the accuracy of Ian's judgements on financial matters, and his utter dependability in meeting deadlines, the initial experience of shock turns quickly into a feeling of deep security.

A further testament to Ian's reputation for dependability and accuracy lies in the fact that he is retained by a leading venture capital company as a financial adviser and board member of investee companies within its portfolio.

5. Perseveres relentlessly

In several categories of SME leadership, we have observed that perseverance characteristically and commonly delivers successful achievement of objectives, sometimes in the face of daunting hurdles. Nowhere is this more marked than in the case of the Manager leader, where from time to time everything that can go wrong does go wrong. Shortages of raw materials, absenteeism and sickness, process breakdown, faulty production, late deliveries, lost contracts, go-slows and strikes, not to mention long hours and weariness, all can accumulate to tax the resilience of the strongest.

Relentless perseverance can overcome all of these, but it is only the true Manager leaders who keep on and on in the face of mounting difficulty. Frustrated, suffering and seemingly fighting a losing battle – but ultimately successful through sheer dogged determination.

3 7-year-old Mark Mills started his first business at 18 and his fourth at 25, with a series of failures and setbacks in between, before developing his first big idea of advertising on the side of postboxes. After severe hard work in launching the concept, he was forced to sell it due to financial constraints. But still he pressed on, and came up with the Cardpoint cash machine business idea that has turned him into a multi-millionaire.

Mark has a sign, 'Failure cannot live with perseverance', over his desk and says:

> "You must not be afraid of failure. If you keep going and never give up, then eventually you will turn it around. You just have to keep your nerve."

LEVERAGING

The Manager leader of an SME knows how to leverage resources so that better outcomes can be achieved than could, or would, be expected by a less competent or ambitious manager. She will pull together the resources to do the job and, if some pieces are missing, will improvise and make do. Her team will be well-motivated, with those responding positively being well-rewarded, but the laggards and incompetents will be quickly fired or re-assigned.

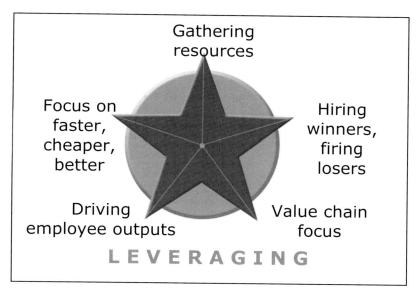

Her focus on, and understanding of, the value chain will enable her to optimise synergies and mutually-re-inforcing activities in all the business' operations and she will drive individual employee outputs, to create a company committed to, and delivering, on the credo, 'faster, cheaper, better'.

1. Gathering resources

P atrick Cooney, with his brother Nicholas, acquired the small Gleeson wholesale company, as an opportunity to get away from a steady life of management consulting, into business and entrepreneurial endeavour with all its risks. There was no grand plan at the outset but, by gathering and leveraging resources, this leader and his family have built a €250 million business that employs over 700 people.

Today, the Gleeson Group owns a range of enterprises, from beverage distribution and wholesaling, to the production of mineral water, cider, soft drinks, cream liqueurs and frozen products. One of its premier brands is Tipperary natural mineral water, which ranks only behind the leading brand Ballygowan in the Irish market.

The history of Tipperary is illustrative of Patrick's determination and ability to leverage resources:

> *"We were drilling a borehole for water which was costing us dearly, at a time when money was scarce. At 300 feet, with a lot of money spent, there was no water and we almost abandoned the project but, after counting our shrinking resources, we gambled on going a further 20 feet and started the drilling again. Six feet later, we hit a 'gusher' and Tipperary water was born".*

Patrick Cooney's strategy is to ensure that the group is well-funded and able to take advantage of the opportunity to acquire assets and leverage their growth.

He is well-aware of the challenge for a private independent SME in competing with multi-national players:

> *"When you only have your own resources to fall back on, you can't afford to make too many mistakes. The iron laws of capitalism are very unforgiving and, if you do make a mistake, you are seriously punished. You have to have resources, not only in the area of finance, but also in self-belief".*

When the enterprise goals have been set, the top team leader has responsibility for analysing the current resources of the firm, matching them with the resources required to deliver the visionary goals and carrying out a gap analysis on areas of difference.

The sources and methodology of acquisition of adequate resource is stated in the business plan, approved by the board or validated by the lone micro leader. But we must not pass too quickly away from discussion of the business plan, whether it is articulated in a 50-page document, or carried in the head of the lone leader.

In the context of resources to fuel a stellar-growth SME, the business plan is analogous to a family shopping-list to fill the refrigerator for the week ahead. Once the fridge is filled, individual tastes and appetites, together with attendances or absences from meals, determines the usage and remaining stock levels of specific items. By mid-week, there are shortages and short-term stock-ups need to be made. When the next 'big shop' is required, the list of staples probably will be broadly similar to the week before, but many items will need adjustment.

Just as the shopping list will be varied from week to week, so the resource business plan is not written in stone. It is the responsibility of leaders to ensure that adequate funds, personnel and facilities are in place so that the company's stellar growth in pursuit of enterprise goals is not slowed by resource starvation.

2. Hiring winners, firing losers

A rsène Wenger, the manager of the world-famous Arsenal football club, maintains that there is little difference between managing a football team and managing a business. He has a degree in economics and was described by Vijay Solanki, head of marketing services at BP Lubricants Europe as 'a management guru in the making,' because of the ideas Wenger suggested he present to the board of BP Castrol Europe.

Wenger maintains that the management problems in both spheres are basically the same, in that the essence is dealing with people and trying to get the best out of them. One of the areas where he has proved his management credentials is in knowing when to change the team and having the courage to take selection decisions in moving even experienced players on, so that new blood can take their place – a job that some business managers shirk, to the cost of their companies. Hiring winners and firing losers is a key contributor to success – whether on the football field or in a business.

Arsène Wenger's example to the leader of an SME is that not only has he assembled one of the most competitive teams in European football, he has done it cost-effectively by using a relatively small squad. He has not flinched from the risky, though highly-profitable, strategy of selling off older players at high prices, while renewing the team with talented youngsters. Notable among the glittering names such as Manchester United, Chelsea, Real Madrid and Benfica, under Wenger's leadership, Arsenal has built its team of talent with comparatively limited resources.

The key to this is the ability to hire well and the courage to move poorer performers on, without being influenced by emotion. Such ability is rare among the leaders of SMEs and they should listen to Wenger's good advice:

"I am not a friend to the players. A friend is someone whom, no matter what he does, I support. I am here to make objective decisions as much as I can, so for me the subjective side of it must disappear".

Leveraging the efforts of people resources by the Manager leader can only be optimised where there is honest, unequivocal transparent objectivity. Arsène Wenger sums it up:

There is no difference between business and football apart from the fact that we are in a job that is public – people can see what we do.

3. Value chain focus

Boards of directors rightly have a focus on the visionary opportunities emerging from changes in the external environment of a company, and this has been described as the 'view from above'. However, for many SME Manager leaders, there is a great deal more to be gained from taking a hard look at the company's value chain and sweating the internal opportunities, by adopting tactics to make the most of what is already there, rather than looking too far afield for inspirational added value. There is likely to be hidden value right within the value chain.

G eoffrey O'Byrne Whyte, the Dublin-based CEO of Air France's CityJet subsidiary, recently presented an interesting alternative 'view from below', which argued convincingly along these lines:

> *"It's probably more important … to have a detailed knowledge of how the organisation works, what its actual potential is and how to invest in that to ensure you get the very best out of it to meet the challenges that you have going forward.*
>
> *A good example of someone who used this approach to his advantage was General Montgomery. He was very successful, but not through any bold strategy – he was no Napoleon. But he trained, rehearsed and prepared his forces before going into battle and, though his strategy was often very simple, he ultimately won out.*
>
> *The view from below needs to take account of what the organisation is capable of. Sometimes strategies need to be watered down to harmonise with the organisation's capability or brand.*
>
> *To succeed, most businesses need to focus on what they know and what they're good at; and do that really well".*

4. Driving employee outputs

In today's pretend world of political correctness, the concept of 'driving employees' towards anything is frowned upon and, sometimes, condemned but, in the real world of business competitiveness, the implementation of this concept arguably does more to preserve the prosperity and rights of employees than any other aspect of the Manager leader's work.

In our experience with stellar-growth SMEs, driven employees generally earn much more than those from whom less is demanded, are better motivated and often are significantly more loyal to their employers.

In the main, this is because a culture of hard work is a much more motivating environment than one in which the contribution of any individual does not seem to carry any real meaning. A recent report on workplace stress in the UK public sector named the chief cause of this condition to be workplace boredom! Who wants to go through life being perpetually bored?

A deeper understanding of psychology demonstrates that employee outputs are driven most successfully by the Manager leader who motivates partly by money, but mostly by meaning.

5. Focus on faster, cheaper, better

Faster, cheaper, better: an unbeatable competitive formula. Two of these can be achieved with hard work, but only in very protected niche markets can all three be delivered in a sustainable way.

The Manager leader searches continually for faster ways to meet customer needs, quicker routes to market, more efficient means of production and speedier, more responsive service. He looks incessantly for approaches that enable him to reduce unit costs of production and make his company the most competitive lowest-cost producer. Quality is an obsession, as he pushes the business towards ever better delivery of services or products.

Tim Roupell started his Daily Bread sandwich company, after being asked to leave his job as a commodities trader in the City. He had noticed that it was very difficult to buy a really good sandwich near where he worked, so he thought that, if he could make a high-quality product – better than the competition – and deliver it directly, and quickly, to offices, he would have a good business.

He started on a shoestring and, despite some scary setbacks over the next 20 years, built a £10 million business that has a Royal warrant to supply the Queen of England:

"I realised that if we offered the best quality and the best service, then people would use us. And that is what has driven us".

PROFITING

All SMEs, all businesses, can only survive over time if they make profits and it is therefore arguably the most important function of any business leader to ensure that this objective is at the top of the leadership agenda. As we discuss the profitability aspect we will be prescriptive as well as allegorical in setting out the behavioural demands of SME leadership.

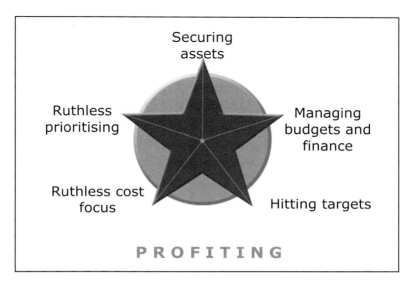

1. Securing assets

Businesses cannot operate or grow without the necessary assets, such as cash, equipment, premises and, indeed, people. It is a key task of the Manager leader to put appropriate assets in place and, as the company grows or its needs change, either to acquire additional resources or to dispose of those no longer required.

Overspend and the business can fail, underspend and it may struggle, but the founder still will have the future opportunity to add to the asset base for growth.

P enny Streeter, founder of the 200-person Ambition 24 Hours recruitment company, has direct experience of all three states. Her first business was born out of her success in working for someone else in the industry, when with supreme confidence she set out by acquiring highly-expensive, opulently-fitted premises:

"We tried to work as hard as we could, but I had overextended on cash from day one, so when the business started to go backwards, my cash-flow projections went right out of the window"

Two years on, she had to close the business, losing all her money. After a difficult period where she had to go into homeless accommodation, Penny decided to have another go but, this time, her strategy on securing the necessary assets was different. No luxury offices and furniture, no fancy cars and she and her mother worked as part-time DJs at weekends to fund the start-up:

"I had no money and I didn't want to go to the bank because I thought they would laugh me out of the door. I learnt not to waste money. The company was run with maximum cost control".

This time, it worked and Penny Streeter built a business, which today turns over in excess of £65 million.

2. Managing budgets and finance

The Manager leader focuses on detail and nothing receives more rigorous attention than budgets and finance. Budgets are carefully crafted by involving the entire team in a bottom-up process, factually-based, using historical experience together with well-researched market projections and, critically, are fully in place before the operating period in question.

We have worked in many situations where the financial budget, perhaps carefully-crafted and factually-based, is not finalised until several months into the period. Often, this due to over-refinement with diminishing returns, or sheer laxity, indicative of serious time-management problems within the company. Either way, this is certainly not the budgetary hallmark of a stellar-growth SME.

The Manager leader will not leave financial management for the sole attention of the company accountant, but will have sufficient understanding of profit and loss accounts, cash flows, balance sheets and other accounting instruments, to add to her intuitive grasp of numbers, putting her in full control of this priority area of responsibility.

Ratios and indicators such as these below, explanations of which can be found in any accountancy or finance textbook, can be invaluable guides as to the SME's effectiveness in the management of its finance:

- Return on shareholders' funds.
- Gearing.
- Earnings yield.
- Dividend yield.
- Earnings per share.
- Market value.
- Financial velocity.
- Profit, actual against budget.
- Margins.
- Liquidity.
- Cash flow.
- Capital expenditure.

3. Hitting targets

Plans and budgets are all very well, but are meaningless in the absence of value-creating performance, both for the ambitious leadership team and for the stellar-growth SME. The targets set in budgets almost invariably show clear value-creation and, in companies run by Manager leaders, there is an obsessional drive to hit or exceed these numbers.

Strong growth often is delivered in situations where beating targets is inspired by the Manager leader and driven deep into the culture of the company.

P owerscreen, now part of the giant Terex Corporation, started as a small engineering business, manufacturing screening equipment for the aggregates and quarrying industries.

The visionary founders continually set demanding targets for all levels of the business, gave people the autonomy to achieve them and then followed through aggressively to ensure their delivery. The result was the stellar growth of Powerscreen in a highly competitive industry, to a position where it is recognised today as a leading worldwide player.

It is still hitting its targets and winning awards, such as 'Exporter of the Year', under the direction of its aptly-named general manager, Damian Power.

4. Ruthless cost focus

Commentators on Ryanair's growth from humble beginnings as an SME minnow start-up, to become one of the most profitable airlines in the world, ascribe much of its success to the ruthless cost focus within the company, inspired by the combative and mercurial Michael O'Leary.

Risky cost pressures created directly by actions such as the following, commonly taken to promote growth, in themselves can seriously prejudice a company's ability to grow:

- Putting in place higher overheads than are specifically required for the current levels of operation of the business as a preparation for expansion and in anticipation of increased activity levels.

- Building service delivery capability or manufacturing capacity ahead of yet unproven demand.

- Increasing stock inventory ahead of demand and thus putting strains on the working capital.

- Skimping or taking short-cuts on product development, so that new products are launched on the market before they are fully ready, thereby incurring rejection and recall costs, on top of the inevitable customer dissatisfaction.

- Paying more attention to volume growth than the need to maintain acceptable gross margins.

- Losing focus by taking on long-term diversification projects.

Michael O'Leary will not be guilty of many of the actions on this list. The SME Manager leader who can maintain an O'Leary approach to costs is an invaluable asset to the company:

5. Ruthless prioritising

Manager leaders are decisive. Being clearly aware of the goals of the business, they prioritise ruthlessly, casting aside ostensibly virtuous non-core projects, to force concentration on those core activities that have been selected as the company's key delivery areas.

But the first priority for the Manager leader lies in what he determines to do with his time and how much of it he will devote – the word is chosen deliberately – to the company. In the words of Duncan Bannatyne, multi-millionaire star of the TV show, *Dragon's Den*:

> *The secret of being successful in business is that there is no secret. Anybody with a spark of intelligence in this country can become a millionaire. You just have to work very hard.*

Of course, there is more to it than that. Daily choices and the right calls have to be made between conflicting priorities, with the mark of the Manager leader being the ruthless ability to discard the lesser priority, despite its inherent worth, and retain the better option.

We often consult with SMEs, whose client lists include many unprofitable customers who should be dumped. But the managers vacillate, seemingly unaware that such parasites are diminishing the strength of the company and taking away from the support services that should be applied to profitable clients.

We go further – we also are guilty of this particular sin and very possibly most of our readers are too.

MANAGER LEADER

Score yourself on each of the behaviours of the Manager Leader below, using the following scoring range:

5 This is one of my outstanding characteristics. I demonstrate this much more than other leaders.

4 This is one of my key strengths. However, I think I could improve on my practice of this behaviour.

3 Sometimes I do this, but not often enough.

2 One of my weaker areas. I rarely demonstrate this. The behaviour does not sit well with me.

1 I don't use this behaviour and doubt if I could.

Total your score. The maximum score achievable is 100, so your score can be expressed as a percentage.

PLANNING		EXECUTING	
Tight controls on process	☐	Delegates work and responsibility	☐
Measures and monitors	☐	Good time management	☐
Effective, thorough planner	☐	Takes responsibility	☐
Driven by facts	☐	Demonstrates dependability / accuracy	☐
Leaves no stone unturned – detail	☐	Perseveres relentlessly	☐

LEVERAGING		PROFITING	
Gathering resources	☐	Securing assets	☐
Hiring winners, firing losers	☐	Managing budgets / finance	☐
Value chain focus	☐	Hitting targets	☐
Driving employee outputs	☐	Ruthless cost focus	☐
Focus on faster, better, cheaper	☐	Ruthless prioritising	☐

Manager Total %

Now transfer your score to page **206**.

8

THE INNOVATOR LEADER

Leadership in innovation is the key factor in ensuring that an SME can sustain its growth over time in ever-changing, highly-competitive markets. Innovation is essential, not only in product or service offerings to customers, but in novel reactions to process, systems, people, management and strategy.

The difficulty in keeping these hard-to-implement approaches to the forefront of thinking in a fast-growth SME is compounded by the fact that most of the individuals who possess the deep insightful skills of the Innovator leader essentially are loners who do not see a pressing need to bring the rest of the team along with their ground-breaking thoughts.

Steve Jobs, in addition to being a great visionary, is the Innovator leader behind the iconic Apple brand. He and his company have had their ups and downs, often as a direct result of Steve's classic innovator 'loner' tendencies, but he has repeatedly initiated and developed world-conquering technology products, both for consumer and corporate markets.

Apple is one of the most recognisable brands in the world and the steady stream of exciting products flowing from its innovation factory – the iMac, iPod, iPhone, MacBook Air, and dozens more – give it the firepower that enabled this upstart, geeky company to acquire the mighty Disney Corporation. All of this was driven by the innovative leadership of Steve Jobs, whose revolutionary innovative idea of a personal computer led him into revolutionising the computer hardware and software industry. Apple changed the world's idea of a computer from a gigantic and complex machine used only by huge businesses and government departments, to a small user-friendly box used by ordinary people.

Jobs had a piercing insight that enabled him to see that the potential development of computing was directly analogous to the earlier establishment, and subsequent growth, of Alexander Graham Bell's watershed invention of the telephone, in the field of communications.

Just before Bell came up with the telephone, telegraph technology had been popular for long-distance communication and some pioneering thinkers suggested putting a telegraph machine on every desk, but this was never going to be a user-friendly idea, as everyone would have had to learn Morse code. A few years later, Alexander Graham Bell filed his first patents for the telephone, and that easy-to-use technology became the standard means of communication.

Steve Jobs saw the future:

> "We're at same juncture; people just are not going to be willing to spend the time learning Morse code, or reading a 400-page manual on word processing. The current generation of computers just will not work any longer. We want to make a product like the first telephone. We want to make mass market appliances. What we are trying to develop is a computer that can do all those things that you might expect, but we also offer a much higher performance which takes the form of a very easy-to-use product".

Very few people have the innovator leadership ability of Steve Jobs, but every SME aiming for sustainable stellar growth must focus actively on developing a competence in this area. Successful innovation, and its output in the form of sustainable competitive advantage, depends on good insights. An insight is a clear, deep perception of a situation, with an intuitive, and often sudden, understanding of its sometimes confusing complexity. For an SME, the most valuable insight is a discovery of something enlightening about the customer, which leads to a differentiated advantage over competitive offerings.

An important lesson for SMEs searching for disruptive differentiating insights is that they are unlikely to find them in focus groups or by asking their customers what they want. Henry Ford, the great innovator leader who did for personal transportation what Steve Jobs did for personal computing, when asked to comment on customer surveys, wryly drawled:

> If I had asked my customers what they wanted, they would have said – a faster horse.

INNOVATOR LEADERS – THE DARK SIDE

The dark side of a leader in any category normally carries its negative connotations, because of how their characteristic actions destructively affect the lives of other people. In the case of Kenneth Lay, he destroyed the lives of shareholders and employees in both Enron and Arthur Andersen, while John Zachary DeLorean dashed the hopes of thousands of people in the then-troubled Northern Ireland.

The example we choose for the dark side of the Innovator leader is Howard Hughes, who exhibited vivid signs of the obsessive loner behaviour so common with this category – but, rather than other people suffering, in fact thousands benefited from the positive effects of Hughes' genius – the chief casualty of the dark side in this case was Howard Hughes himself.

F or the last 20 years of his life, this brilliant innovative genius lived in eccentric isolation, finishing eventually in squalor, despite his billions of dollars of wealth.

Howard Hughes had the good fortune to be the eldest son of the man who patented the Hughes oil drilling bit, at a time when oil exploration was growing rapidly, and at 19 years of age, he inherited a business that made him one of the richest people in the world.

But he wasn't just a rich man's son. He was also a mathematics prodigy, a talent he was to put to good use in a vast range of design applications during his career, including creating the design for a bra for Jane Russell, who starred in his film classic *The Outlaw*.

Hughes was a genuine Innovator leader in engineering through his global eponymous company. Then, silent and, later, talking movies followed, where he made several box-office smashes.

He also took the lead in aircraft design, with his ultimate triumph being the acclaimed 'Spruce Goose', the largest plane of its time. Though it flew only once, it is recognised as a technical leap forward that laid the groundwork for many of the breakthroughs that occurred in the post-war period leading up to the establishment of mass-transport jet aviation.

In his earlier years, Howard Hughes inspired great loyalty from his followers and they took tremendous pride in being associated with the phenomenal revolutionary achievements of this superstar Innovator leader. However, he was badly injured in a plane crash, after which his intimidating, though inspirational, volatility was exacerbated, assuming a form of extreme obsession, and he slid progressively into a state of dark reclusive isolation.

Living in sealed-up hotel penthouses, he and his entourage of mainly Mormon helpers ran his vast business interests, while he retreated ever deeper into a state of irrationality. The behaviour traits that made him one of business history's major innovators and leaders became so obsessive that they utterly destroyed him. He died a 'madman' in 1976 at the age of 71: sadly, a flawed genius.

The special leadership behavioural characteristics of the Innovator leader are the ability to solve, to create, to renew and to change.

SOLVING

Note this statement by PricewaterhouseCoopers in the firm's new millennium review of innovation around the world:

> *"The most valuable organisations of tomorrow will be idea-rich, have a culture where innovation is embedded as a core capability and value, and will embrace new and unusual ways of fostering innovation."*

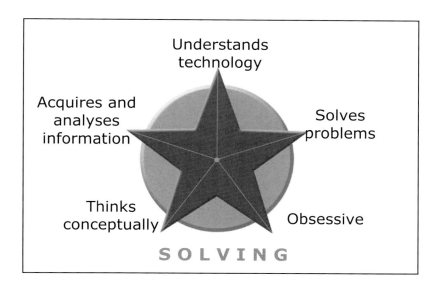

1. Understands technology

Having a deep understanding of the relevant technology in the industry concerned is a mark of the effective leader of innovation. Steve Jobs and Bill Gates today cannot be described as leaders of SMEs but, at one time, they certainly were and they both demonstrated Innovator leadership, based on first principles, hands-on knowledge of software and computers.

Technology leaders in the search for better ways of making things work may come up with the next big thing or maybe, because of their technical orientation, they may develop a product in search of a market that doesn't exist.

Starting with a deep understanding of technology, and allying that to an appreciation of unfulfilled customer needs, is the classic route for successful innovation. This is illustrated in star rally-driver James Leckey's engineering expertise being married to his accurate perception of the needs of disabled children, leading to business innovation that is profitable for Leckey Design and life-changing for the users of its products.

2. Solves problems

Certain people have a real knack when it comes to solving problems and the SME Innovator leader will be thinking in the same way as Sean Quinn, not only about products and technology, but about every complexity that arises in the daily operation of the company.

Innovator leaders can look at a problem and, if the road to a solution requires logical, linear thinking for incremental gain, they can quickly go down that road but, if it requires lateral thought, they have the unique ability to come up with solutions that enable step-change transformations, such as those delivered by Steve Jobs and Bill Gates.

A t a more mundane product level, Andrew Schofield from County Down faced a problem when trying to design and build a maintenance-free house. He was unable to source an alternative to the ubiquitous, but aesthetically uninspiring, PVC bargeboards for the roof-ends so, in the spirit of a true innovator, he set to work in a search for a novel solution.

After extensive research and experiment, supported by various award bursaries, Andrew produced the *RoofBLOCK*, which is maintenance-free and fits comfortably with traditional building aesthetics. It is now an established product with distribution throughout Ireland and the UK.

3. Obsessive

Real innovation is not easy and demands an obsessive concentration in order to turn dreams into reality, a point that is well-made by the innovator heroes of history: Edison, Bell, Dunlop, Fleming and, in more recent times, Gates and Jobs, all focussed obsessively on their innovative business goals, some at great cost to their personal lives.

Obsession is a common trait among the Innovator leaders of SMEs and is well-exemplified in the career of James Dyson, who, while he now owns a company with billions of dollars of sales, in common with every innovator entrepreneur spent the tough years of his life in leading SMEs.

J ames' first foray into entrepreneurship, after a successful design
career, was the launch of the *Ballbarrow* and a number of
products using derivatives of the idea.

In 1976, when renovating his house, he realised that his vacuum
cleaner was losing suction during use. From that moment on, his
obsession became the motive force that drove him and his team
through 5,127 prototypes and five years of disappointments, until
he perfected the *Dual Cyclone* vacuum cleaner.

James' obsessive determination was further called on to beat back
the desperate, and sometimes underhand, attacks of the market
leaders on his innovative disruptive technology's threat to their
previously-unassailable market domination.

4. Thinks conceptually

Concepts of the mind are the tools that Innovator leaders use to
simplify and make sense of the complexity that confuses lesser
thinkers and, paradoxically, it is comparative simplicity of thought
that conveys the greatest solving power.

Failure to use concepts results in becoming bogged down in
stultifying detail and this clogging of thought flexibility results in
an absence of lateral thinking, which delivers the answer to so
many problems.

Concepts are the foundation of scenarios or alternatives, where
several outcomes can be considered and the Innovator leader is
unconcerned if they appear vague, blurred or imprecise. That is
precisely their function; the concrete detail will be added later, after
conceptual thinking has presented a broad way forward.

W rightBus, based in Ballymena, Northern Ireland, is the UK's
leading independent supplier of public transport buses.
Throughout its history, from formation in 1946, this family-
owned company has built its success on innovation, winning the
prestigious Manufacturing Excellence Award for Product
Innovation in 2006 and 2007.

The conceptual thinking, which has no doubt contributed to their
award successes, is evident in WrightBus having pioneered the

development of low-floor buses in the UK and, more recently, realising the concept of the world's first hybrid diesel/electric double-decker bus, currently running between Palmers Green in North London and London Bridge.

The concepts, which began with founder Robert Wright in 1946, were maintained, and added to, by his son, William Wright. The future now lies in the capable hands of Mark Nodder, who regards his appointment as MD and concept leader of this successful family company as *"a rare privilege"*.

In April 2008, this innovative family-owned company won a £125 million contract to supply new vehicles to a leading UK and North American bus operator, First Group, in the face of competition from 24 rival bus manufacturers. Mark Nodder attributes the success to Wright's skilled workforce, its world-class manufacturing facility and significantly, its strong technical and design department:

> *"This is one of the biggest orders ever placed in Irish or British bus manufacturing history. It took us six months to win this contract. First Group were looking not only for value for money, but innovative design that delivered high performance and advanced technology"*.

5. Acquires and analyses information

It is a well-established fact in the theatre of war, that the possession of superior intelligence or information on the enemy of itself is a distinct combat advantage. If that knowledge is analysed carefully, and turned into powerful battle strategies that can be implemented with boldness, then overwhelming victory is assured.

While business is seldom a zero-sum game as in the field of warfare, the analogy largely holds good, placing significant importance on acquiring and analysing timely and accurate information, so that the SME is equipped with the armament of strategic or tactical competitive advantage.

On the contrary, lack of information breeds insecurity, and insecurity discourages innovation. It is the job of Innovator leaders to drive an open culture that encourages information search, kaleidoscopic thinking and courageous active analysis for everyone in the company, and not just the few who carry the dedicated responsibility for research.

CREATING

Some people have the unique ability to operate their mental faculties simultaneously at different levels, in much the same way as described by F. Scott Fitzgerald:

> *The test of a first-rate intelligence is the ability to hold two opposed ideas in mind at the same time and still retain the ability to function.*

The innovator leader has a creative mind that passes this great author's test.

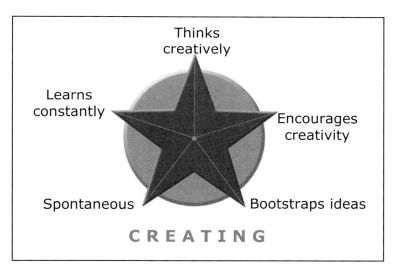

1. Thinks creatively

The brain of a truly creative person will generate ideas at great speed in response to a situation. Less imaginative individuals will react to the many concepts with limited, though perhaps rational enough, thoughts, such as:

- *"It's a good enough idea but ...".*
- *"It won't work – we tried it last year".*

- *"It won't work – we have never tried it before".*
- *"OK, but it is going to be very expensive to implement".*
- *"It will be difficult to get that past the board".*
- *"This might breach the regulatory codes".*
- *"There are a number of complications with this".*
- *"It is not as simple as all that".*
- *"Our competitors will be able to copy it".*

This negativity is extremely irritating to the Innovator leader, but does nothing to stem the flow of creative thinking from the fertile brain.

2. Encourages creativity

The ability of creative leaders to attract others, simply because of their aura of excitement, can create a positive atmosphere of enthusiasm around them and, hence, can lead to an explosion of creativity within a group.

Their conceptual fluency stimulates others to think in the same way and, in discarding a line of thought at the press of a button, to take a lateral leap towards a loosely-related frame of reference, they encourage their colleagues to go after similarly-flexible mental risks, thus benefiting the entire process. It may appear capricious and unstructured but it is intuitively powerful, in that it brings creative contribution from the entire motivated team.

3. Bootstraps ideas

Because an idea or innovation is nothing if it is never implemented, many concepts within SMEs remain dreams never to be fulfilled, due to lack of funds or a champion. Yet others see the light of day, in spite of these drawbacks. The difference lies with the bootstrapping creative leader who overcomes immense difficulty to make the seemingly-impossible happen.

The term 'bootstrapping' refers to the difficulty of a person gaining any altitude by heaving on their own bootstraps and, while in a literal sense this is a quite impossible task, the analogous successful implementation of ideas where there are no identifiable resources does really occur. The creative leader will find a way where others just give up.

T o stretch the analogy, a 14-year-old boy making jam in his granny's kitchen would hardly appear to have boots at all, never mind bootstraps to pull on yet, within four years, Fraser Doherty's jam was selling in 360 Tesco and Waitrose supermarkets throughout the UK.

The idea was to use grape juice to sweeten the fruit instead of refined sugar or artificial sweeteners, thus allowing *Superjam* to be presented as a rich, but healthy, alternative to the products of the food giants behind *Hartley's*, *Bonne Maman* and *Robertson's*.

The teenage Fraser bootstrapped his innovative fledgling business out of his parents' kitchen and into a factory, where he is geared up to production of 40,000 jars a month – and he is still only 18 years old.

4. Spontaneous

Acting on a hunch, trusting in instinct, making the instant decision and regularly surprising the team are all marks of the creative Innovator leader. The risks of getting things wrong are huge and only mitigated by the leader's experienced judgement but, when the spontaneity is proven to deliver the right answer, the reputation and power of the leader soars.

Joey Reiman, CEO of BrightHouse, an Atlanta-based 'ideation corporation', says that creativity has more to do with what people feel than what they think. His approach to innovation is to :

"… do heartstorming rather than brainstorming".

D avid Salisbury has a conservatory manufacturing business with over 100 employees, which started spontaneously from the day this former student of physics and deep-sea diver was asked to help in putting together a conservatory. He describes it as a revelatory experience:

"I was hooked by the way the roof went together. We had to order double-glazed units of different shapes, so, using my physics

background, I got out my pen and worked out all the angles and glass sizes. So that when we took the conservatory out to site, it just fitted together".

David felt excited at how his physics knowledge worked in this context and, spontaneously, he decided he could use it further by designing and building his own conservatories.

5. Learns constantly

Taking the time to learn, to reflect, to analyse and to retain can be difficult for a hard-pressed SME leader but the creative leader recognises its priority and, like Sean Quinn, can find a way to absorb the facts, signals, trends and vital snippets of information that add to relevant learning, while in the middle of intense and often chaotic activity.

The key is openness of mind and an ability to select relevance, while discarding dross.

In the 1990s, Peter Senge popularised the 'learning organisation'[24] and, more recently, Noel Tichy has presented a lengthy tome on the teaching leader.[25] Both approaches have great merit but the requirements of innovation in an SME demand learning-leadership – constantly.

There is an inherent vulnerability in the individual who is prepared to admit to learning constantly, as that state implies a lack of knowledge and understanding, but self-confident Innovator leaders rightly brush this thought aside.

When we were children, our natural curiosity motivated us to explore and learn unselfconsciously, simply because we wanted to. It is a similar inquisitive cultural approach that the Innovator leader will encourage within their SME.

Such acceptance and search for learning does not require the payment of bonuses or award of stock options – leave that to the

---

[24] Peter M. Senge, *The Fifth Discipline: The Art & Practice of the Learning Organisation*, Transworld, 1990.

[25] Noel M. Tichy, *The Cycle of Leadership: How Great Leaders Teach their Companies to Win*, HarperBusiness US, 2004.

Googles and Microsofts – but it does require innovative, creative leadership.

RENEWING

Constant renewal is a successful surviving organisation's response to a constantly changing environment, but it doesn't happen without pro-active leadership. There is a strong tendency in all organisations to get to a settled steady state, where change is the exception rather than the disturbing tiresome rule and it takes the input of motivational energy, to overcome this dangerous competitiveness-sapping trend.

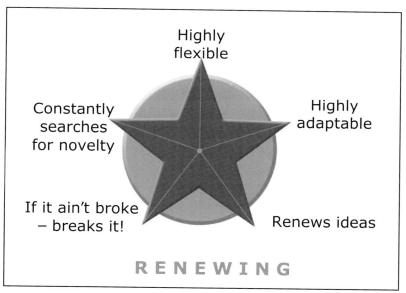

1. Highly flexible

As we age, our once-athletic flexible bodies lose the suppleness that enabled the enjoyment of demanding sports. While the degenerative process can be postponed to some degree by regular exercise and careful diet, it and the onward journey of our own life-cycle ultimately brings us to a stage where we lose the ability to participate in strenuous, competitive physical activity.

SMEs also are subject to the impact of life-cycle degeneration but the effects leading to inflexibility need not apply with the same inevitability, where vigorous innovative renewing leadership is in place. Generally, inflexible companies are 'led' by inflexible leaders and flexible companies are led by flexible leaders; this is a vital lesson for the leader.

In the pre-Thatcher era in Britain, when workers were represented by monolithic, inflexible trade unions, many large companies were sclerotic dinosaurs moving inexorably towards extinction, brought on by their own slow-moving inflexibility. Such weakness, as part of a national lethargy in many countries throughout Europe, was also extended into thousands of SMEs.

One of Margaret Thatcher's greatest contributions to the economic wealth of all the citizens of the UK – and some would argue to the entire citizenry of Western Europe – was to put legislation in place that created a flexible industrial environment and, out of that, flexible competitive companies.

2. Highly adaptable

Flexibility is the physical ability to bend and move easily, while adaptability is the mindset and skills capability that allows implementation of a new or renewed activity.

Adaptation is a component of innovation and while, in the area of products, it tends to deliver incremental improvement rather than step-change, as an activity, it can bring great benefit to a product range.

Adaptation, however, brings greatest value where the Innovator leader herself demonstrates adaptability and, by extension, supports the skills training that transmits it to the workforce. Where adaptability is present in a company, its innovative capacity is greatly increased.

Adaptability is a close relation of flexibility, but the significant difference lies in flexibility being the willingness and freedom to change, while the value of adaptability lies chiefly in the possession of the skills and capabilities to perform different tasks day-to-day.

3. Renews ideas

When companies search for innovations in order to renew the product line, to refresh their offering or to increase competitiveness, there is a tendency to look for the 'next new big thing', but the Innovative leader also will trawl constantly through the existing product range or ideas bank, where in practice the best breakthroughs may be found.

D on Lewin was born in poor conditions in the East End of London before World War II and, through a series of entrepreneurial ventures, built his wealth until, at the age of 40 in the mid-1970s, he was able to afford a Rolls Royce.

A few years earlier, he had opened the first of a chain of greeting card shops, the success of which had delivered the dream car, but even with competitors entering the market, he saw still greater possibilities in the future and applied his fertile mind to renewal of ideas to keep him one step ahead.

In addition to the traditional birthday, Christmas and occasion cards, Don introduced new card-giving occasions to reflect social changes, with cards for gay couples, 'divorce cards' – with both commiseration and congratulation wording – and cards with innovative captions, like 'To Mum and Dad on your wedding day'.

Don was well aware of the need to renew ideas in order to stay ahead, and this is still a feature of the massive retail business now run by his son and daughter:

> *"We need to be constantly on the lookout in this business. It is a fashion business and, to keep in front of everybody else, we need to be coming up with all these new ideas all the time".*

4. If it ain't broke – breaks it

General Colin Powell puts a different slant on an old slogan, which strongly supports the renewing leader's drive to enervate the SME's innovative thrust:

> *'If it ain't broke, don't fix it' is the slogan of the complacent, the arrogant and the scared.*

Charles Handy, in *The Elephant & the Flea*,[26] makes a strong argument that the time to innovate and change a business formula is around the peak of its success, when the company and personal morale is at its highest, rather than when decline has set in and the people have taken on the attitude of defeat:

> *Long-lasting organisations have to find ways to start second curves, before the first curves peak. That's hard to do. It means recognising, in the midst of a run of success, that it can't last forever and that, paradoxically, now is the time to start investigating alternatives. It is easier to do that when the need for change is obvious, when the curve is obviously heading downhill. But that is just the time when morale is low, resources are depleted, and leaders are discredited – the worst conditions for any radical thinking.*

Apple is a company that lives by this philosophy. According to *Fortune* magazine, Apple's approach is:

> *... to put every resource it has behind just a few products and make them exceedingly well. Apple is brutal about culling past hits: the company dropped its most popular iPod, the Mini, on the day it introduced the Nano (a better product, higher margins – why dilute your resources?).*[27]

Handy also argues that there are earlier, perhaps minute, signs that all may not be well. The Innovator leader will be acutely attuned to spotting these signals, so that direct action can be taken.

A perhaps apocryphal story that illustrates the point is the famous statement by Joe Kennedy, shortly before the 1929 Wall Street crash, when he told how, on being given investment tips in an elevator by a bell-hop, he went straight to his broker and sold all his shares, turning his total assets into cash. What a call, what timing, what acute listening to a faint signal.

---

[26]   Charles B. Handy, *The Elephant & The Flea: Looking Backwards to the Future*, Hutchinson, 2001.

[27]   'What Makes Apple Golden?' by Betsy Morris, *Fortune*, 3 March 2008.

5. Constantly searches for novelty

Pioneering is an exciting, if sometimes dangerous and uncomfortable, occupation for most people, but there are those for whom it is the very reason they get out of bed in the morning, just to see 'what's new?'. These novelty-seekers are Innovation leaders. They are people who, rather than being overwhelmed by a full mailbox, can hardly wait to open their emails to see what novel opportunities await the application of their curiosity.

O wen Barratt started work as a builder's labourer, saved every penny and then embarked on a dizzying series of early businesses before forming CVD, which he has turned into the largest diamond-drilling company in Scotland, with 110 employees.

His success has not blunted his appetite for novelty. He has expanded his interests into a diverse portfolio of activities, from recruitment to IT, but with the common denominator that he knows and trusts the people running the new activities. This is a vital touchstone and allows the Innovator leader to be involved in novel projects, while significantly de-risking the initiatives:

"I would never invest in a project if I didn't know the person behind it – no matter how lucrative the opportunity. Setting up new companies is the fun part of business for me".

Owen's interest in novelty is not confined to business. For his next project and novel experience, in support of the Anthony Nolan Trust, he is heading for Nepal to climb Mera Peak, at 21,246ft the highest of the Himalayan trekking mountains.

CHANGING

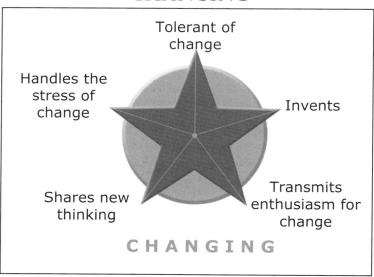

1. Tolerant of change

The SME leader who can create a culture that accepts change has given the company a powerful, continuing opportunity to maintain competitive advantage in its marketplace. Tolerance of change demands a self-confident maturity on the part of all members of staff, together with deep trust of the leadership. Trust initially is relatively shallow in any situation, but deep trust is based on repetitive positive experience over time so, paradoxically, it is the very consistency of the Innovator leader's approach that creates the culture of change tolerance.

> Grafton, the international employment solutions provider, is an Irish company, which under the innovative leadership of James Kilbane and Ken Belshaw has enjoyed stellar growth. It currently turns over well in excess of £100 million and, building on past international success, plans to open 17 new offices in 2008, including new branches in Hungary, India, Slovakia and Turkey.

> James Kilbane, when asked to describe his typical day, illustrates the Innovator leader's hectic schedule as he drives his organisation's change agenda:

"There isn't really a typical day, but rather a typical week. Monday morning sees me check in at Dublin airport on a direct flight to one of our 18 countries. I generally embark on visits lasting five days with a return flight to Ireland, either last flight on a Friday or first flight on a Saturday morning. Considering our hectic rate of expansion, this has been an extremely regular occurrence."

2. Invents

Invention is the hallmark of the changing Innovator leader. The ability to invent brings with it the positioning aura that gives authority to great leaders such as Steve Jobs or James Dyson and, earlier, Thomas Edison, Alexander Graham Bell and Henry Ford.

The Binding Site is a 24-years-established low-profile biotech company, with sales of £38 million in diagnostic cancer tests. A spin-out from Birmingham University, it is still run by one of the founder/inventors, Professor Jo Bradwell.

Professor Bradwell, the majority shareholder in this significant company, has overseen its steady growth in a sector that has produced significant high-profile failures and exaggerated claims over the years. His understated approach in building on a high-integrity invention without fanfare has enabled this SME to achieve solid profits year-on-year and, more importantly to Jo Bradwell, its products have saved thousands of lives.

3. Transmits enthusiasm for change

Change can be imposed by coercion, but its effect will only last as long as the pressure is applied. To get real sustainable change requires enthusiasm on the part of all participants; leadership is the key to its transmission and maintenance.

Michael Deane's Michelin Star restaurant in Belfast was voted the best in Ireland in 2007 and he has several other highly successful ventures in Northern Ireland. His has been no instant success – it has been over 20 years in the making – but, from the earliest days of Deane's, he has had the courage to change and the ability to transmit enthusiasm for change to his entire team.

In 2006 and 2007, he has completely re-furbished his flagship restaurant, opened a new bar and grill at Queen's University and evolved a novel eating-out experience, with the development of the Deane's Vin Café & Deli Bistro.

Michael states clearly that, while he is the owner and personal face of the business, its success is a team effort and his team responds enthusiastically to the constant challenges.

> *"My game plan was always to surround myself with the best young talent – and to know when to get out of the kitchen! I'm still the captain of the ship, but now I have the chance to patrol the decks of each of the restaurants every night.*
>
> *This is a hard business. You have to be on top of your game all the time to meet your customer's expectations and to constantly re-invent yourself and your offering to meet the needs of the times."*

4. Shares new thinking

The generative power of shared thinking is graphically illustrated in the spreading of new ideas through blogs and special interest sites on the Internet, where a new thought can catch on and within a very short period of time can become a worldwide phenomenon. The Innovator leader can galvanise her company by using this power.

L ara Morgan's Pacific Direct company turns over in excess of £17 million, selling imported goods to four- and five-star hotels. With factories in China and the Czech Republic, Lara spends a lot of time travelling – to the sometimes consternation of her staff, due to her insatiable reading of business books and articles when she is away.

> *"My first three employees would shake in their boots because I would come back from a trip with two or three books where I had turned over a corner of the pages and scribbled all over them. The first thing I would do after trips was photocopy pages of these books and put them in their in-trays with a note saying 'You might be interested in this, do have a look at this, read this.'"*

Lara puts her success down to her desire to learn and share her learning with the Pacific Direct team, so that the business gets full value from her innovator leadership:

"I read business books passionately like a lunatic when I travel. I have just come back from a trip to Italy and, on the way, I read business magazines and, when I came back, I put 18 different sheets of photocopied articles into people's trays. There was an article on rent negotiation, there was one on new technology so I put that in the IT guy's tray. I invest in my staff a lot."

5. Handles the stress of change

Any incident or process variation that demands a response from us, brings an element of stress, whether it is mild, as in the case of our usual morning paper being unavailable, or severely damaging, where a loved one is seriously ill. The Innovator leader who, on the one hand, has the role of engendering change must also have the resilience to cope with its stressful pressures, while setting a confident example to the rest of the team.

Deirdre Bounds learnt from an early age to cope with the changes that life can bring, having been brought up in an environment where nothing positive came along without a struggle. Her basic can-do attitude helped her through a variety of jobs but her first venture into business on her own was proving difficult, until a friend advised her to break out of her frightened shell and move forward.

This she did and her 1-to-1 SME business has succeeded and grown ever since, driven by the coping mantra that Deidre adopted at the age of 11:

"I remember deciding that I was going to succeed in everything I did, and the only person who could change things was me."

INNOVATOR LEADER

Score yourself on each of the behaviours of the Innovator Leader below, using the following scoring range:

5 This is one of my outstanding characteristics. I demonstrate this much more than other leaders.

4 This is one of my key strengths. However, I think I could improve on my practice of this behaviour.

3 Sometimes I do this, but not often enough.

2 One of my weaker areas. I rarely demonstrate this. The behaviour does not sit well with me.

1 I don't use this behaviour and doubt if I could.

Total your score. The maximum score achievable is 100, so your score can be expressed as a percentage.

SOLVING		CREATING	
Understands technology	☐	Thinks creatively	☐
Solves problems	☐	Encourages creativity	☐
Obsessive	☐	Bootstraps ideas	☐
Thinks conceptually	☐	Spontaneous	☐
Acquires and analyses information	☐	Learns constantly	☐

RENEWING		CHANGING	
Highly flexible	☐	Tolerant of change	☐
Highly adaptable	☐	Invents	☐
Renews ideas	☐	Transmits desire for change	☐
If it ain't broke – breaks it!	☐	Shares new thinking	☐
Constantly searches for novelty	☐	Handles the stress of change	☐

Innovator Total % ☐

Now transfer your score to page **206**.

9

THE WILD-CARD LEADER

Wild-Card leaders defy precise description and they certainly do not fit neatly into the categories of our leadership model. But, just like the more conventional leader-types, these driven, idiosyncratic, unpredictable types can run very successful – sometimes outstandingly successful – companies.

If truth were told, maybe there is a bit of the Wild-Card in all entrepreneurs and perhaps it is that whiff of wildness and danger, which really sets them apart from the bulk of business managers. For that reason, and to complete our observations on the SME leaders we have known and seen, we look at three larger-than-life characters.

Each of the examples we use – Ryanair's Michael O'Leary, the late buccaneering entrepreneurial giant Sir James Goldsmith and the irreverent publishing mogul Felix Dennis – built their stupendously successful careers running stellar-growth SMEs, before achieving legendary status.

WILD-CARD LEADERS – THE DARK SIDE

It is difficult enough to pin down the 'typical' Wild-Card leader to describe in positive tones. We have to be doubly careful in quoting examples that illustrate the dark side of such individuals – but dark side there is. It can be exhibited in ways that show some Wild-Card leaders to be cruel, deceitful and capricious in the extreme.

The Wild-Card leaders we have met, while displaying many of the aggressive characteristics of combativeness and outrageously surprising behaviour, usually have basic values of honesty and integrity, despite their otherwise non-conformist volatility. Indeed, in many cases, we are aware of great acts of kindness they have performed, which belies their more usual reputation.

When considering the dark side of the Wild-Card leader, we are referring to specific types of unscrupulous characters – none of whom appear in this book – whose value systems do not include the common decencies, let alone honesty and integrity.

For this reason, and on the good advice of our lawyers who remind us that, in addition to their capricious vindictiveness, these types are extremely litigious, we will not give a specific named example – dead or alive – of a dark-side Wild-Card. We just point out that they certainly do exist in the world of SME entrepreneurship and that, if you see one appearing, get out of their way.

MICHAEL O'LEARY – WILD-CARD

To get the flavour of the approach of such off-the-wall successful people, we quote from a 2005 *Guardian* report by Andrew Clark:[28]

> *Travellers stuck in traffic jams on the busy approach road to Dublin airport occasionally catch a glimpse of a luxury Mercedes speeding past them along the bus lane. A scruffy, weather-beaten figure sits in the back clad in a checked shirt and faded jeans.*

> *The boss of Ryanair, Michael O'Leary, is a man in a hurry. Such is his impatience with anyone in his way that he paid £4,000 for a taxi licence for his private car, equipped it with a meter and uses it to evade congestion between his Mullingar home and Ryanair's Dublin airport headquarters.*

> *When challenged on his abuse of this licensing loophole, O'Leary was utterly unapologetic, boasting that the pointless meter showed an average fare of £82 for his journey to work: "Last time I checked, this was a democratic republic. As long as I pay my taxes, I'm free to do with my money what I like".*

> *O'Leary, 44, is among Ireland's richest men, with an estimated fortune of £280m. His airline is a staggeringly successful business: in 1985, it employed 51 people and shuttled 5,000 passengers between Britain and Ireland. It is now Europe's most profitable carrier, with 2,600 staff and a*

---

[28] Copyright Guardian News & Media Ltd 2005.

network of 233 routes stretching as far afield as Poland, Finland and Lithuania. It expects to carry 35 million travellers this year.

But, with every penny earned, the former public schoolboy nicknamed 'Ducksie' by his classmates acquires an ever more awkward reputation. "I don't give a shite if nobody likes me", he told one interviewer, stressing that he was a businessman through and through. "I am not a cloud bunny, I am not an aerosexual. I don't like aeroplanes. I never wanted to be a pilot, like those other platoons of goons who populate the air industry".

Casual abuse is O'Leary's stock-in-trade. He has described the European Commission as "morons", the airport operator BAA as "overcharging rapists". Britain's air traffic control service is "poxy", British Airways are "expensive bastards" and travel agents are "fuckers" who should be "taken out and shot".

This week, the green lobby was in O'Leary's sights. Rattled by pressure over aviation's contribution to climate change, a coalition of airlines formed a "sustainable aviation group", claiming to take the concerns of environmentalists seriously. It wasn't O'Leary's style and Ryanair was isolated in the industry in refusing to offer its support.

Concerns about climate change, O'Leary maintained, are nothing to do with him. He proudly declared that Ryanair intended to increase its emissions of carbon dioxide, adding that, if his customers were worried about the environment, his advice was straightforward: "Sell your car and walk".

He said his rivals' attempts to reach out to the greens were fraudulent: "The sustainable aviation group, God help us, is another bunch of lemmings shuffling towards a cliff edge".

In the eyes of environmentalists, O'Leary has become public enemy number one. Richard Dyer, aviation campaigner at Friends of the Earth, says: "Michael O'Leary is insulting the public's intelligence and his honesty about his desire to increase Ryanair's carbon emissions doesn't make it any more acceptable. His contempt for the impact of his actions on the world's climate shows how important it is that the aviation industry is brought under control."

Transport 2000 described aviation as a "massive national banana skin", which could cancel out all other efforts to cut greenhouse gases, adding: "When we hear that the leader of a low-cost airline cares little about the impact of his company on the environment, that really is very worrying".

The pressure group Future Forests calculates that each Ryanair passenger journey equates to an emission of 0.6 tonnes of carbon dioxide. To offset its annual impact on the climate, the airline would need to plant 16.5m trees.

But, behind all the outrage and hand-wringing, there is a case for the defence. Over the last five years, Ryanair has spent more than £5bn renewing its Boeing 737s. While it once flew 25-year-old jets, it now has one of the most modern fleets in the world. The new planes produce 50% fewer emissions than their predecessors, burn 45% less fuel and make 45% less noise.

O'Leary's pre-occupation is simple: low fares. Ryanair's average ticket costs €41 (£27), compared with €62 (£41) on easyJet or €268 (£178) on BA. He argues that any emissions trading schemes or taxes on aviation fuel will hit his passengers far harder, in proportionate terms, than those on BA or Lufthansa.

"This is high-fares airlines getting together and pursuing policies for blocking competition", he says.

Although an unreconstructed Thatcherite in all things economic, O'Leary regards himself as the champion of the common man - a "jumped-up Paddy", as he once described it, in challenging the airline establishment.

With its rock-bottom prices, Ryanair can claim to have drastically shaken up travel. It was the first budget airline this side of the Atlantic.

To its fans, O'Leary's airline has broadened the horizons of millions of people: it is Ryanair which ferries Poland's carpenters and plumbers to seek work in London. It is Ryanair which made Essex accents commonplace on the promenade at St Tropez. It is Ryanair's cheap flights which made it affordable for Britain's chattering classes to snap up second homes in the Loire valley, Burgundy and Provence.

Yet O'Leary's claims to the so-called Irish "poor voice" do not quite ring true. Born into an affluent farming family, he attended Clongowes Wood, the so-called Eton of Ireland. He went on to Trinity College and qualified as an accountant at KPMG.

His wedding in 2003 to a former banker, Anita Farrell, was attended by Ireland's great and good, including the racing millionaire J.P. McManus, the European commissioner Charlie McCreevey and the deputy prime minister, Mary Harney. For a honeymoon, the couple flew business class to Mauritius.

Siobhán Creaton, author of an unauthorised history of Ryanair, believes O'Leary's middle-class background explains a lot: "He got the best education money could buy but a lot of his peers at school would have been the sons of people like [the newspaper magnate] Tony O'Reilly, who stood to inherit the family fortune. He had nothing much to take over from his family."

She sees his hectoring style as a throwback to his rural upbringing: "At heart, I suppose he's a farmer. He behaves, in some ways, like a farmer does when he's going to a market to sell his cattle."

The rocketing Ryanair passenger numbers, which so distress environmentalists, are down to a mixture of savvy marketing and brutal cost control. Although fares can be as low as 99p, Ryanair squeezes an average of £2.50 out of each passenger in food, drink, car hire bookings and other 'ancillaries'. Bottled water on board costs almost £4 a litre.

O'Leary's ideas to save money have included scrapping window blinds and seat pockets and even banning check-in luggage. Customer service can be dismal – a judge ordered Ryanair to compensate a disabled man last year after it refused to foot the bill for a wheelchair.

His frugality can reach the point of pedantry. Crew have to pay for their own training, uniforms and meals. Head office staff must supply their own pens and are even forbidden from charging their mobile phones at work. O'Leary refuses to recognise trade unions – the Irish union Impact claims it has 270 victimisation cases outstanding between Ryanair pilots and management.

Shay Cody, Impact's deputy general secretary, says: "He seems to be absolutely determined to resist unions at any price. In doing so, he's created, ironically, a very well-organised pilot body".

O'Leary's pugnacity extends to the world of politics. He has a rancorous relationship with Bertie Ahern, partly down to arguments over facilities at Dublin airport.

In recent years, O'Leary has made more than £145m from selling shares in Ryanair. What he does with the money is something of a mystery: he leads a relatively modest life on his loss-making cattle estate, some 40 miles west of Dublin, although he is said to have a penchant for art and antiques. He is a big rugby fan, but his most expensive habit appears to be dabbling in horse breeding.

Green lobbyists insist Ryanair's growth is unsustainable, although it shows little sign of slowing any time soon. Passenger numbers are forecast to jump by 26% this year, overtaking British Airways' worldwide total.

The relentless aggression is similarly irrepressible and was on show again at a press conference this week. Ryanair's marketing manager, Sinead

Finn, noted that she was the only woman addressing a roomful of male journalists. "I wouldn't be too sure", interrupted O'Leary. "There's someone here from The Guardian *and you can never tell with them".*

In the two and a half years since Andrew Clark wrote this report, O'Leary has confirmed his Wild-Card characteristics time after time.

One week after the Irish flag-carrier Aer Lingus was privatised in early 2007, he pounced and totally wrong-footed his competitors, the aviation industry and the Irish Government, by carrying out a completely unexpected audacious raid on Aer Lingus shares. This blind-side coup saw Ryanair ultimately amass a powerful stake of 29% in the company.

O'Leary is the epitome of the seemingly-fearless, outrageous Wild-Card leader, who cuts a reckless swathe through, over, under and around those generally accepted taboos that form the rules of the game in business and political life.

He accomplishes his objectives in belligerent fashion, but often with tongue-in-cheek boyish devilment, which, while perhaps entertaining for the non-involved, is undoubtedly excruciating and embarrassing for his unfortunate targets.

He remains the outrageous, combative, surprising and persistent Wild-Card Michael O'Leary.

SIR JAMES GOLDSMITH – WILD–CARD

During the second half of the 20th century, James Goldsmith was one of the most ebullient characters in the field of international commerce. But, as a precocious shooting-star entrepreneur at the age of 24, he was within hours of bankruptcy and complete failure.

In three years, he had built the French *Laboratoires Cassene* from one employee to 400 but he had expanded too far, too fast and, by the evening of 9 July 1957, he knew that bills to be presented to the bank the following morning could not be paid. He was bankrupt.

The prologue to *Tycoon*, Geoffrey Wansell's biography of Goldsmith,[29] gives a picture, most of it in his own words, of this Wild-Card's reaction to a situation that would have shattered most people.

> *"In the circumstances I slept very well. It was over. I was finished."*
>
> *When he woke the next morning, he did not bother to get up or shave. It was not that he was particularly depressed; there was simply nothing to be done, and no point in going to the office. Eventually, to cheer himself up, he decided to go out to lunch.*
>
> *"At a corner kiosk I bought the* Paris-Presse, *to see if my bankruptcy had made the newspapers. But when I opened it, the first thing I saw were big headlines saying 'BANK STRIKE'. I couldn't believe it. It galvanised me. I realised I had extra time."*
>
> *Goldsmith went into immediate action and phoned* Laboratoires Roussell, *his company's biggest competitor in the pharmaceutical industry in France.*
>
> *"During the next 18 days or so, I managed to sell almost everything else to* Roussell. *They gave me £120,000, and I went away on holiday to Spain for two months to recuperate."*
>
> *Thirty years later, the man who was to become a billionaire and 'the most powerful predator in the stock market jungle' told his friends:*
>
> *"It was a spectacular example of luck. The gods stopped scowling that day. I still took reckless risks after that – I can't say it taught me not to. But I never considered any success certain again."*

From that day forth, he continued to rely on his own intuition – and his own luck. And, by doing so, he became one of the most extraordinary, flamboyant and unconventional tycoons in history, as well as one of the richest men the world has ever known.

---

[29]   Geoffrey Wansell, *Tycoon: Life of James Goldsmith*, Grafton Books, 1987.

FELIX DENNIS – WILD–CARD

Michael O'Leary and James Goldsmith both started on their Wild-Card SME careers with some advantage: in O'Leary's case with a first-class education and sterling contacts, while Goldsmith not only had the education but also started with the momentum of a financial blue-blood heritage.

It was harder for Felix Dennis, a failed, penniless R&B singer, whose only asset was a burning ambition to get rich – very rich.

In his witty book, *How to get Rich*,[30] which contains a wealth of valuable down-to-earth advice, Felix displays some of the unconventional and counter-intuitive characteristics of the Wild-Card leader:

> *In 1972, I persuaded a jolly young lawyer I had met to act for me. His name was Bernie Simons. I had no money to pay him but perhaps my chutzpah amused him … Next I persuaded a close friend, Dick Pountain, to join me as co-director and production manager. There wasn't much in the way of a salary on offer but Dick came all the same.*

Felix describes the office where he started the business that became a £500 million publishing giant:

> *Three rooms at the top of the most rickety stairs I had ever climbed. The building had been badly damaged in the Blitz and never properly rebuilt. The last tenants had been breeding puppies there in straw pens. It took a long time to get rid of the stink of puppy shit. The place was a total dump but, at least, we had an office.*
>
> *I launched half a dozen magazines about a new fad called 'personal computing' in the 1980s, even though British magazine retailers and wholesalers at the time were unanimous in their belief that 'nobody will ever buy them'. Those magazines have earned me tens of millions of pounds in the last 25 years and are still earning me money today. Conventional wisdom is usually right. But when it is wrong, it can offer quite extraordinary opportunities for those too stubborn or inexperienced to pay attention to well-meaning naysayers.*

---

[30] Felix Dennis, *How to Get Rich*, Ebury Press, 2006.

Anyone not busy learning is dying. For as long as you foster a willingness to learn, you will ward off sclerosis of the brain and hardening of the mental arteries.

The only way to deal with fear is to cosy up to it. To look it in the eye and pump its hand. To translate its negative energy into adrenaline. To harness it. To laugh with it, rather than at it.

WILD-CARD LEADER

Score yourself on each of the behaviours of the Wild-Card Leader below, using the following scoring range:

5   This is one of my outstanding characteristics. I demonstrate this much more than other leaders.

4   This is one of my key strengths. However, I think I could improve on my practice of this behaviour.

3   Sometimes I do this, but not often enough.

2   One of my weaker areas. I rarely demonstrate this. The behaviour does not sit well with me.

1   I don't use this behaviour and doubt if I could.

Total your score. The maximum score achievable is 100, so your score can be expressed as a percentage.

OUTRAGING		FIGHTING	
Attacking the 'status quo'	☐	Readiness to retaliate	☐
Offending the 'great and the good'	☐	Aggressive in the extreme	☐
Creating news through shock	☐	Tenaciously defending the firm	☐
Offending political correctness	☐	'Us' against 'the rest'	☐
Making enemies and not caring	☐	Using dirty tactics, if necessary	☐

SURPRISING		PERSISTING	
The ability to charm	☐	Refusing to be defeated	☐
Doing the unexpected	☐	Relentless ambition	☐
Using frequent humour	☐	Not taking 'No' for an answer	☐
Unbalancing the competition	☐	Succeeds against the odds	☐
Pulling the 'rabbit out of the hat'	☐	Crashing and resurrecting	☐

Wild-Card Total %

N.B.   The scoring for Wildcard Leader is not included in the STAR model. Few leaders will adopt the 'Outraging' and 'Fighting' approaches of the Wildcard leader but the 'Surprising' and 'Persisting' behaviours are certainly worth consideration.

ERRATA

Enter your **personal** scores for Visionary (page 85), Team-Builder (page 119), Seller (page 148), Manager (page 172) and Innovator (page 194) leadership behaviours on **page 208**.

Enter your **company** scores (pages 210-214) on **page 215**.

Enter your **sector** scores (pages 217-221) on **page 222**.

10

EVALUATION

YOUR PERSONAL STAR SHAPE

Chapters 4 to **8** cover in detail 100 facets of leadership that, in ideal fulfilment, will characterise STAR leadership behaviours in a stellar-growth SME. The 20 facets of the Wild-Card leader (**Chapter 9**), while not included in the model, are there for consideration, in light of the fact that they do exist in the real world. We will all encounter Wild-Card leaders from time-to-time.

In these chapters, you have identified the extent that you yourself behave in line with each facet or characteristic. Rigorously marking yourself, being ruthlessly honest as you insert your numbers in the tables, will help you to make a judgement on your personal leadership profile and competences.

Bring forward your percentage scores for each vector from the previous chapters and mark them on the STAR diagram on the next page to see the shape of your own leadership STAR.

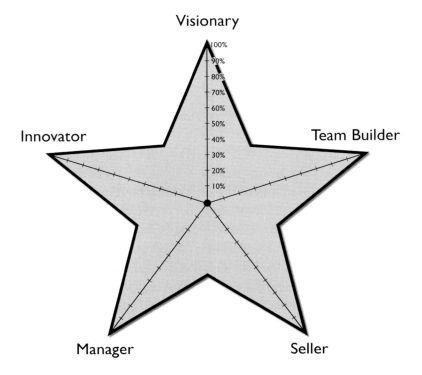

STAR EVALUATION IN YOUR COMPANY

Note that this next section is about overall leadership behaviours of the top team – not only about you as leader.

The purpose is to assess the effectiveness of your top team in covering the leadership behaviours required to deliver stellar growth for your SME.

This section should be completed in workshop session by the entire top team. Maximum benefit will be derived if the team can identify specific members of the team who have unusually positive strengths against particular leadership behaviours.

Mark the tables on the following pages for this assessment in the same manner as you did for your own personal STAR profile. Score your company's top team on each leadership vector, using the following scoring range:

5   The company is superb at this and this behaviour is evident in all that the top team does. It is a key competitive advantage for them.

4   The company is strong at this. The top team seems to see it as important.

3   The company exhibits this behaviour from time-to-time.

2   The company does not appear to put much emphasis on this behaviour.

1   The company does not do this.

Total your company's score. The maximum score achievable is 100, so the score can be expressed as a percentage.

VISIONARY LEADERSHIP BEHAVIOURS IN YOUR COMPANY

VISIONING	
Thinks entrepreneurially	☐
Stretches boundaries	☐
Dreams big dreams	☐
Thinks 'outside the box'	☐
Bold in Vision	☐

STRATEGISING	
Sets ambitious goals	☐
Spots opportunities	☐
Plans methodically	☐
Researches meticulously	☐
Builds new concepts	☐

ENERGISING	
Inspires people	☐
Has high drive and ambition	☐
Demonstrates passion	☐
Very hard worker	☐
Looks to the future	☐

DECIDING	
Takes big risks	☐
Takes hard decisions	☐
Tough-minded	☐
Handles ambiguity	☐
Faces reality	☐

Company Visionary Total %

Now transfer your score to page **213**.

TEAM-BUILDER LEADERSHIP BEHAVIOURS IN YOUR COMPANY

SELECTING

Attracts followers, leads by example ☐

Removes poor followers ☐

Matches people to tasks ☐

Delegates authority ☐

Establishes order and discipline ☐

COMMUNICATING

Talks, and listens, to people ☐

Knows the people well ☐

Communicates openly / honestly ☐

Holds regular informal meetings ☐

Gives consistent feedback ☐

HARMONISING

Creates shared vision ☐

Confronts conflict ☐

Demonstrates compassion ☐

Breaks down cliques ☐

Is tolerant and kind ☐

MOTIVATING

Rewards individual performances ☐

Turns setbacks into opportunities ☐

Creates a positive optimism ☐

Sets challenging tasks ☐

Is demonstrably courageous ☐

Company Team-builder Total %

Now transfer your score to page **213**.

SELLER LEADERSHIP
BEHAVIOURS IN YOUR COMPANY

PROSPECTING

Deep industry knowledge ☐

High customer focus ☐

Good listener ☐

Assiduous researcher ☐

Persistent worker ☐

BONDING

Sophisticated and attractive ☐

Empathetic and trusting ☐

Bearing, presence and charisma ☐

Humorous and engaging ☐

Powerful presenter of self and ideas ☐

CLOSING

Strong negotiator ☐

Powerful seller and bargainer ☐

Assertive attitude ☐

Highly self-confident ☐

Decisive closer ☐

NETWORKING

Great contact base ☐

Busy networker ☐

PR awareness ☐

Highly respected ☐

Very well-known ☐

Company Seller Total %

Now transfer your score to page **213**.

MANAGER LEADERSHIP IN BEHAVIOURS IN YOUR COMPANY

PLANNING

Tight controls on process ☐

Measures and monitors ☐

Effective, thorough planner ☐

Driven by facts ☐

Leaves no stone unturned – detail ☐

EXECUTING

Delegates work and responsibility ☐

Good time management ☐

Takes responsibility ☐

Demonstrates dependability / accuracy ☐

Perseveres relentlessly ☐

LEVERAGING

Gathering resources ☐

Hiring winners, firing losers ☐

Value chain focus ☐

Driving employee outputs ☐

Focus on faster, better, cheaper ☐

PROFITING

Securing assets ☐

Managing budgets / finance ☐

Hitting targets ☐

Ruthless cost focus ☐

Ruthless prioritising ☐

Company Manager Total %

Now transfer your score to page **213**.

INNOVATOR LEADERSHIP BEHAVIOURS IN YOUR COMPANY

SOLVING

Understands technology ☐

Solves problems ☐

Obsessive ☐

Thinks conceptually ☐

Acquires and analyses information ☐

CREATING

Thinks creatively ☐

Encourages creativity ☐

Bootstraps ideas ☐

Spontaneous ☐

Learns constantly ☐

RENEWING

Highly flexible ☐

Highly adaptable ☐

Renews ideas ☐

If it ain't broke – breaks it! ☐

Constantly searches for novelty ☐

CHANGING

Tolerant of change ☐

Invents ☐

Transmits desire for change ☐

Shares new thinking ☐

Handles the stress of change ☐

Company Innovator Total %

Now transfer your score to page **213**.

The 'Shape' of leadership behaviours in your company

Bring forward the percentage scores for each of the leadership vectors and mark them on the STAR diagram below to show the current shape of leadership behaviours in your company.

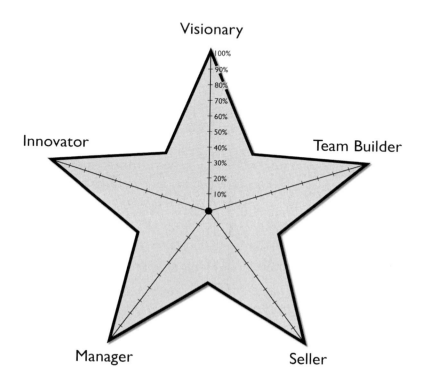

STAR EVALUATION IN YOUR BUSINESS SECTOR

Now you need to consider the competitive leadership needs of best-practice competitors in the market(s) in which your SME competes.

Here, you are measuring the level of importance of the key leadership behaviours necessary for the best companies to gain and sustain competitive dominance, in the business sector within which your SME competes.

The benchmarks for this exercise are the behaviours of the market leaders in your sector. Identify them and assess their behaviours.

Mark the tables on the following pages for this assessment in the same manner as you did for your own personal STAR profile. Score the market leaders in your sector on each leadership vector, using the following scoring range:

5   The market leaders are superb at this and this behaviour is evident in all that they do. It is a key competitive advantage for them.

4   The market leaders are strong at this. They seem to see it as important.

3   The market leaders exhibit this behaviour from time-to-time.

2   The market leaders do not appear to put much emphasis on this behaviour.

1   The market leaders do not do this.

Total the market leaders' score. The maximum score achievable is 100, so the score can be expressed as a percentage.

We believe that the most effective and accurate way to complete this part of the exercise is by involving other members of your top team.

VISIONARY LEADERSHIP NEEDS IN YOUR SECTOR

VISIONING NEEDS

Thinks entrepreneurially ☐

Stretches boundaries ☐

Dreams big dreams ☐

Thinks 'outside the box' ☐

Bold in Vision ☐

STRATEGISING NEEDS

Sets ambitious goals ☐

Spots opportunities ☐

Plans methodically ☐

Researches meticulously ☐

Builds new concepts ☐

ENERGISING NEEDS

Inspires people ☐

Has high drive and ambition ☐

Demonstrates passion ☐

Very hard worker ☐

Looks to the future ☐

DECIDING NEEDS

Takes big risks ☐

Takes hard decisions ☐

Tough-minded ☐

Handles ambiguity ☐

Faces reality ☐

Sector Visionary Needs Total %

Now transfer your score to page **220**.

TEAM-BUILDER LEADERSHIP NEEDS IN YOUR SECTOR

SELECTING NEEDS

Attracts followers, leads by example ☐

Removes poor followers ☐

Matches people to tasks ☐

Delegates authority ☐

Establishes order and discipline ☐

COMMUNICATING NEEDS

Talks, and listens, to people ☐

Knows the people well ☐

Communicates openly / honestly ☐

Holds regular informal meetings ☐

Gives consistent feedback ☐

HARMONISING NEEDS

Creates shared vision ☐

Confronts conflict ☐

Demonstrates compassion ☐

Breaks down cliques ☐

Is tolerant and kind ☐

MOTIVATING NEEDS

Rewards individual performances ☐

Turns setbacks into opportunities ☐

Creates a positive optimism ☐

Sets challenging tasks ☐

Is demonstrably courageous ☐

Sector Team-builder Needs Total %

Now transfer your score to page **220**.

SELLER LEADERSHIP NEEDS IN YOUR SECTOR

PROSPECTING NEEDS

Deep industry knowledge ☐

High customer focus ☐

Good listener ☐

Assiduous researcher ☐

Persistent worker ☐

BONDING NEEDS

Sophisticated and attractive ☐

Empathetic and trusting ☐

Bearing, presence and charisma ☐

Humorous and engaging ☐

Powerful presenter of self and ideas ☐

CLOSING NEEDS

Strong negotiator ☐

Powerful seller and bargainer ☐

Assertive attitude ☐

Highly self-confident ☐

Decisive closer ☐

NETWORKING NEEDS

Great contact base ☐

Busy networker ☐

PR awareness ☐

Highly respected ☐

Very well-known ☐

Sector Seller Needs Total %

Now transfer your score to page **220**.

MANAGER LEADERSHIP NEEDS
IN YOUR SECTOR

PLANNING NEEDS

Tight controls on process ☐

Measures and monitors ☐

Effective, thorough planner ☐

Driven by facts ☐

Leaves no stone unturned – detail ☐

EXECUTING NEEDS

Delegates work and responsibility ☐

Good time management ☐

Takes responsibility ☐

Demonstrates dependability / accuracy ☐

Perseveres relentlessly ☐

LEVERAGING NEEDS

Gathering resources ☐

Hiring winners, firing losers ☐

Value chain focus ☐

Driving employee outputs ☐

Focus on faster, better, cheaper ☐

PROFITING NEEDS

Securing assets ☐

Managing budgets / finance ☐

Hitting targets ☐

Ruthless cost focus ☐

Ruthless prioritising ☐

Sector Manager Needs Total %

Now transfer your score to page **220**.

INNOVATOR LEADERSHIP NEEDS IN YOUR SECTOR

SOLVING NEEDS	
Understands technology	☐
Solves problems	☐
Obsessive	☐
Thinks conceptually	☐
Acquires and analyses information	☐

CREATING NEEDS	
Thinks creatively	☐
Encourages creativity	☐
Bootstraps ideas	☐
Spontaneous	☐
Learns constantly	☐

RENEWING NEEDS	
Highly flexible	☐
Highly adaptable	☐
Renews ideas	☐
If it ain't broke – breaks it!	☐
Constantly searches for novelty	☐

CHANGING NEEDS	
Tolerant of change	☐
Invents	☐
Transmits desire for change	☐
Shares new thinking	☐
Handles the stress of change	☐

Sector Innovator Needs Total %	

Now transfer your score to page **220**.

The 'Shape' of best-practice leadership behaviour in your sector

Bring forward the percentage scores for each leadership need and mark them on the STAR diagram below to show the leadership behavioural shape required for your company to compete optimally in your business sector.

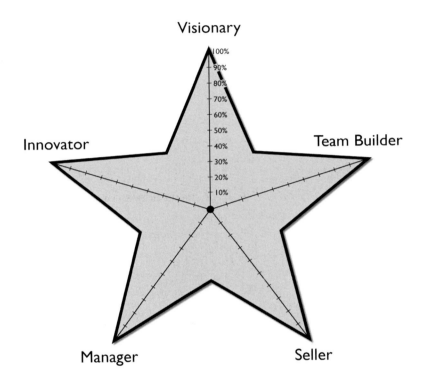

NEXT STEPS

Having completed these evaluations, for yourself, your company and your sector, you now need to identify the gaps where you and your SME need to improve your leadership capability in your search for stellar growth. There are just a few simple steps to do this.

Company gaps

- Plot on a flip chart the STAR shape of best-practice leadership behaviours in your sector.
- Overlay the STAR shape of leadership behaviours in your company.
- Analyse the gaps – in your company's favour and against.

Personal gaps

- Plot on a flip chart the STAR shape of best-practice leadership behaviours in your sector.
- Overlay your own personal STAR shape.
- Analyse the gaps – in your favour and against.

For further information, go online to **www.linkubator.com/star**.

We can arrange direct face-to-face consulting support on use of the STAR model, together with leadership behavioural training and development where required. Details on the website.

Now that you have identified the gaps in behaviour between the market leaders in your sector and your own company / yourself, you can take action to close the gaps.

This book recognises that you, as the leader of an SME, and your colleagues within the top team, face many of the same challenges that confront the leaders of much larger organisations than your own.

Your significant additional difficulty is that you must wrestle with such challenges without the deep support systems of a multi-national and, yet, often these are the very organisations against which you have to create competitive advantage in order to ensure your firm's very survival.

However, there are also advantages in being smaller. Agility, innovation, speed of response and entrepreneurial attitude always will deliver competitive differentiation.

Above all, it is the continuing and consistent practice of positive, situationally-appropriate, leadership behaviours that enable a company to punch above its weight and to achieve stellar growth: delivering reward to the workforce, shareholders, leadership team, the SME leader and all stakeholders in the enterprise.

Do let us know your thoughts on the STAR model, the book and on SME leadership issues in general at **www.linkubator.com/star**.

Over to you!

INDEX

OAK TREE PRESS

is Ireland's leading business book publisher.

It develops and delivers
information, advice and resources
to entrepreneurs and managers –
and those who educate and support them.

Its print, software and web materials
are in use in Ireland, the UK, Finland,
Greece, Norway, Slovenia, India,
Bangladesh and Sri Lanka.

OAK TREE PRESS

19 Rutland Street
Cork, Ireland
T: + 353 21 4313855
F: + 353 21 4313496
E: info@oaktreepress.com
W: www.oaktreepress.com